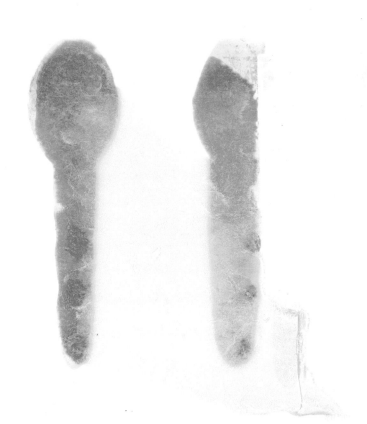

SUFFRAGE AND RELIGIOUS PRINCIPLE:

Speeches and Writings of Olympia Brown

edited by
DANA GREENE

3020

The Scarecrow Press, Inc.
Metuchen, N.J., & London
1983

Frontispiece: Courtesy of the Schlesinger Library, Radcliffe
College

Library of Congress Cataloging in Publication Data

Brown, Olympia, 1835-1926.
    Suffrage and religious principle.

    Bibliography: p.
    Includes index.
    1. Women--Suffrage--United States--Collected works.
2. Feminism--United States--Collected works.   3. Women's
rights--United States--Collected works.   I. Greene, Dana.
II. Title.
JK1896.B7625 1983   324.6'23'0973   83-20129
ISBN 0-8108-1665-2

Manufactured in the United States of America

For my four daughters:

Justin, Kristin, Lauren, and Ryan

May they have the fire of Olympia Brown

CONTENTS

A special debt of gratitude is owed the Schlesinger Library on the History of Women, Radcliffe College, for use of its collection and for financial assistance to carry out this research. I also gratefully acknowledge the following: Bert Hartry for her work in cataloging the Olympia Brown Papers; Ernest Cassara for reading the introduction; Allan Seaburg, Edward Blankman, and Ralph Schmidt for bibliographic assistance; Holly Allison and Margarita Duran for their help in transcription of manuscripts; and Richard Roesel, my husband, whose good humor and encouragement make all the difference in my life. It is hoped that this anthology will reveal the power of Brown's insight and her consistent dedication to religious principle and the cause of women.

Dana Greene
St. Mary's City, Md.
January 1983

In the history of the long struggle for the female franchise in the United States, the name of Olympia Brown will appear occasionally in a footnote documenting the Kansas Campaign of 1867 or the formation of the New England Woman's Suffrage Association in 1868. To relegate Brown to this academic obscurity is not only to diminish her sustained contribution to the achievement of the female franchise but to leave unexplored the intimate connection between feminism and religious insight which is so obvious in her life and so essential in understanding the role of religion in social reform movements in nineteenth-century America.

Olympia Brown, a Universalist minister and the first denominationally ordained woman in the United States, [1] worked for over half a century for the cause of woman's suffrage. Most typically, she is seen as a suffragist who happened to be a Universalist. Such a juxtaposition of her political and religious commitments is an inversion of her priorities. Universalism was not incidental to her life; it was central and all pervasive. This peculiarly American religious tradition provided Brown the principles from which she interpreted her world and the goals toward which she marshalled her considerable energies and talents. It gave her a sense of self-worth, designated a life work for her, sustained her through bitter and trying times, and helped her understand the meaning of American history.

The writings and speeches of Olympia Brown offer a unique understanding of what it meant to be a religious person in late nineteenth- and early twentieth-century America. For Brown it meant to be actively dedicated to the advance of the goal toward which all history moved, the realization of "democratic Christianity." The way Brown chose to live her religion was in single-minded dedication to one objective, the enfranchisement of women. For her this was no puny goal, but one of enormous magnitude and meaning.

In nineteenth-century America there was nothing distinctive about religious commitment prodding one to involvement in social reform. Abolitionism, temperance, penal reform, and pacificism all drew heavily from the ranks of the religious committed. The woman's rights movement, however, did not generally find adherents among this same group. In fact, by the late nineteenth century that movement was seen as anathema by many who claimed to be religious and it increasingly relied on rationalistic rather than religious arguments to make its case.

Brown was one who extended the purview of reform by the religiously committed to include woman's rights. She did this at great price. Although Universalists generally were not hostile to this inclusion, neither were they supportive, and from less liberal denominations there was condemnation. She was also strangely out of sync with many of her colleagues in the suffrage movement. Although she shared with them a specific goal, the enfranchisement of women, neither in her presuppositions about reality, her motivational commitment, her personal style, nor her tactics did she find much support from them. She measured all things by religious principle and the fact that others did not was frustrating to her. It is clear in her writings and speeches that her constancy and dedication to suffrage against terrible odds were possible because of her commitment to principle. It is also clear that it was such unbending commitment which flawed her ability to lead the movement in a more creative way.

Olympia Brown's ninety-one years stretched across the turbulent history of late nineteenth- and early twentieth-century America. Raised on the Michigan frontier by a deeply religious mother who wanted educational opportunities for her eldest child, Brown was sent East to attend Mount Holyoke Female Seminary in 1854. She disliked the stultifying life there, the useless rules and especially the prevailing religious belief in a wrathful and punishing God.[2] Intent on refuting this doctrine, she studied scripture and found confirmation of the universality of divine love, the belief transmitted to her in childhood by her mother, who had read the works of Hosea Ballou.[3] In 1856, when she could stand Mount Holyoke no longer, she enrolled in Antioch College, a co-educational institution under the enlightened leadership of Horace Mann. The years at Antioch were formative for her. In an environment relatively free from sectarianism, she became convinced that the notion of eternal punishment was irrational and pernicious and that she must work to

counteract its influence.[4]   The preaching of Antoinette Brown
at Antioch inspired her.   "It was the first time I had heard
a woman preach," Brown wrote, "and the sense of victory
lifted me up.   I felt as though the Kingdom of Heaven were
at hand."[5]

By the time she finished her studies at Antioch in
1860, she had decided to enter the ministry.   She was accepted at the Canton School of Theology at St. Lawrence Uni-
versity[6] and was ordained by the St. Lawrence Association
of Universalists in Malone, New York, in 1863.[7]   An educated woman, driven by extraordinary commitment and gifted
with enormous energy, Olympia Brown began her work as a
full-time pastor in 1864 at Weymouth, Massachusetts.   To
her commitment to the ministry she added another labor, work
for suffrage.   This dual role as pastor and suffragist would
occupy her for more than twenty years.

In 1866 she attended her first woman's rights meeting
and toured New York State with Susan B. Anthony.   A year
later, at the urging of Lucy Stone and Henry Blackwell, she
campaigned for woman's suffrage in Kansas.   She went to
Kansas not as a minister but as a suffragist.   Blackwell's
claim that through suffrage work Brown might "do more to
destroy sectarianism and emancipate the human soul than by
any other means"[8] apparently resonated with her.   The hos-
tilities toward the female franchise ran deep in Kansas.   The
campaign introduced her to the rough and tumble of politics,
but Brown claimed that winning one third of the vote was a
victory for principle.[9]

After the Civil War, Brown joined the Equal Rights
Association, the national organization formed to secure rights
for blacks and women.   She quickly realized that the question
of female suffrage was not being adequately addressed by the
association.   In 1868, she called for the formation of an entirely separate organization, the New England Woman's Suffrage Association, to be dedicated specifically to securing the
female franchise.[10]

When the National and the American Woman Suffrage
Associations were formed in 1869, Brown walked a narrow
line between them, supporting both the Stanton-Anthony faction, with whom she felt stronger sympathy, as well as Lucy
Stone and the Boston women.   She frequently attended the conventions of these associations and later served as Vice-Pres-
ident of the National Woman Suffrage Association.

By 1870, Brown had decided to leave her church in Weymouth for a new pastorate in Bridgeport, Connecticut, where she hoped to have a "larger field of usefulness."11 During that time she married John Henry Willis, a Bridgeport businessman and former trustee of the Weymouth church. Her mother and friends urged her not to marry on the grounds that it would restrict her preaching, but she apparently found Willis a supportive partner. She claimed he assisted rather than interfered with her work, shared all her undertakings and "always stood for the right."12

In 1878, Brown accepted a position as Pastor of the Church of the Good Shepherd in Racine, Wisconsin, moving her husband and two young children with her. She immediately became involved in suffrage work there. In 1884, she was elected president of the Wisconsin State Woman Suffrage Association, a position she held for the next twenty-eight years.

Brown's dual commitment to full-time ministry and to suffrage work ended in 1887, when she resigned as pastor of the Racine church. Although she continued to preach on a supply basis for the next eleven years, it was the suffrage issue which would principally claim her energies for the decades to come. Brown's writings offer no clear explanation for this decision. There is no indication that she was frustrated with her work as a minister. Rather over the years she became more deeply involved in suffrage work and by 1887 she saw that there was much to be done in Wisconsin and no one ready to do it.13 This natural evolution of her work was possible because in her mind there was no discontinuity between the general goals of spreading Universalist principles as a minister and the realization of a particular goal, the equality and liberty of women, through suffrage work.

The franchise was for Brown the "insignia of citizenship," the intrinsic right belonging to every citizen, inherited by those born here and claimed by those who chose to live in the United States and accept its values.14 It was the instrument by which one made known one's wishes to society15 and the right on which all other liberties depended and were made safe.16 She felt the impact of extending the franchise to women would be far-reaching. It would elevate the status of women and thus improve society. Enfranchised women would give better example to their children, and better-born and -raised children meant an improvement of the race.17

The female franchise would insure that the values of home, school, and church had a full hearing in society. To continue to exclude women from the ballot would fuel corruption and restrict government to representing business interests.[18]

It was particularly galling to Brown that at a time when swarms of immigrants were awarded the franchise, all American women were denied it.[19] The "serfs of the Old World," the "ignorant" and the "drunk" could become citizens and vote after only a brief residence, while educated and pure American women remained disenfranchised. While Brown's rhetoric on this issue seems shrill, it is false to argue that she opposed the extension of suffrage to immigrants. "America is not for Americans," she said, "it is for Humanity."[20] To her, the mistake was not that suffrage had been extended too broadly, but that it had not been extended broadly enough. Suffrage, she felt, should be given to immigrants after an appropriate period of residence and should be extended to all women citizens, who with their intelligence and purity could counter trends which might otherwise erode the Republic.[21]

Brown claimed that denying women the right to vote was based not on constitutional principle but only on custom. The framers of the Constitution believed that the "people" had the right to vote, she argued. It was only in the state constitutions that the qualification of sex was imposed on voters.[22] She advocated a return to the first principles of the Constitution which clearly supported the broadest democracy.[23] The tactic to be used to gain female suffrage was not an amendment to the federal constitution or state constitutions, or a court decision, but a federal law passed by the House of Representatives mandating that females be permitted to vote in the election of members of the House, the only democratically elected branch of government. Since the House could legitimately determine the qualifications for the electors of its membership, only a federal law, she argued, was necessary to insure women the vote.

When the National and the American Woman Suffrage associations merged in 1889, Brown refused to join, ostensibly because of the organization's emphasis on winning suffrage on the state rather than the national level. Instead, in 1892 she founded the Federal Suffrage Association, an organization through which she advocated her goal of the passage of a federal law to authorize the female franchise in the election of members of the House of Representatives. This was the beginning of her increasing alienation from other suffragists.

What she later called "the great desert of woman's suffrage,"24
the period 1890-1910 was a difficult one for her both in terms
of suffrage work and her personal life.   The death of her
husband in 1893, of her mother in 1900, and the burden of
running the family business alone for seven years after Willis's death, all took its toll.   She was discouraged about the
progress of suffrage work as well.   There was indifference
toward the suffrage issue, recruits were down and money was
short.   Her book Acquaintances: Old and New Among Reformers, published in 1911, illustrates this discouragement
and her nostalgia for the vigor of the early suffrage movement.   She was particularly irritated by the new suffrage recruits, whom she claimed lacked the "immortal fire" of the
courageous "old pioneers."25

        The fragmentation of the suffrage movement was also
debilitating.   Brown's own Federal Suffrage Association, the
history of which she recorded in Democratic Ideals: A Sketch
of Clara B. Colby, was now in competition with the National
American Woman Suffrage Association.   Yet of the two,
Brown believed it was the Federal Suffrage Association that
had on the national level "kept the flag flying" on the suffrage
issue during those long and difficult years at the turn of the
century.26   In Wisconsin, where Brown had had so much influence, bitter factionalism grew up among a number of rival
suffrage associations.   In 1912, after a poorly handled state
campaign ended in defeat, Brown resigned from her twenty-
eight-year tenure as president of the Wisconsin Woman's Suffrage Society claiming that this would allow for new leadership to emerge.27

        Although Brown had hoped that the achievement of the
female franchise would be swift, she recognized after years
of effort that this work was a part of a long and difficult
struggle.   "The full history of woman suffrage," she wrote
in 1914, "cannot be written for it is the history of the grad-
ual development of the human race.   It is the climax of the
long struggle toward emancipation."28   The part of the struggle in which she had participated had indeed been long, ardu-
ous, and discouraging.   In reflecting on these difficulties and
the failures of the movement she wrote:

                It is difficult to work for a great and unpopular
                cause for years without some degree of discourage-
                ment.   The number of people who will work for a
                principle which seems to the superficial to have no
                personal interest for them is very small; the great

> multitude failing to understand the motives or even
> the action of reformers are generally unjust in their
> judgment and cruel in their criticism. While the
> advocates of the cause, being human and liable to
> mistakes, are often unwise in the policy they pur-
> sue. This is particularly true of the woman's
> rights cause.[29]

By 1913, Brown had found new hope and enthusiasm for
woman's suffrage. She joined the Congressional Union, later
called the Woman's Party, and with this ally she worked for
the final passage of the suffrage amendment. The militancy
of the Congressional Union women and their insistence on a
federal amendment are what renewed her.[30] In 1920, when
the Nineteenth Amendment was passed, Olympia Brown was
the only "old pioneer" who was alive to see the fruits of the
labors of earlier suffragists. Brown was eighty-five years
old at the time. She recognized that the female franchise
would not solve all questions of justice for women; there was
much yet to be done. However, she turned her still active
mind to another issue, the ending of militarism and the establishment of peace. At first blush this seems like a radical departure for one so dedicated to the single cause of female suffrage. In truth, this new direction followed logically
from her previous concerns.

As Brown saw it, the major problem confronting society in the second decade of the twentieth century was increased militarism, a trend she believed would quickly erode
the full democracy she had worked so long to achieve. She
felt the war with Germany had to be fought out to the end;
it was a struggle against the power of the state over the individual. But militarism, which seemed to be engulfing the
nation, had to be curbed.[31] It was to the newly enfranchised
women that she appealed specifically:

> I could wish that the whole womanhood of America
> would join and with one voice denounce the whole
> military system, compulsory service, military
> training, and the expenditure of millions of the
> people's money for munitions of war. Surely the
> united voice of all the women would be heard. Mil-
> itarism would be swept away and our country con-
> secrated to "peace on earth, good-will to men."
> Such an accomplishment would be worthy of the
> great struggle and sacrifices that have been made
> to give women the ballot.[32]

Brown's attacks against militarism should not be con-
strued as unpatriotic. Her life-long dedication to the ideals
of the Declaration of Independence and her defense of the Republic will not support this charge. Yet for Brown, patriotism was not the highest ideal. "There is something grander
than patriotism, it is faith in the unity of humanity and this
is a love greater, more dazzling, more alluring than love of
one's own land."[33] It was to this higher ideal, the unity of
humanity, that Brown addressed her final years. Since militarism divided humanity, she felt it must be fought against.
Work for peace among nations bolstered that unity and hence
must claim her support. In 1919, she wrote that education
to the brotherhood of mankind was necessary to insure peace,
and she urged Universalists to lead the way by sending missionaries to the Old World to bind up the wounds of war, heal
the broken-hearted, and comfort those who mourned.[34]

In 1926 Olympia Brown died, her life having come full
circle. An evaluation of her ninety-one years is difficult.
For decades she worked doggedly for the female franchise
with little personal support from within the suffrage movement and less from without it. This dedication was possible
because she totally believed that she was working for principles which would necessarily be realized. This dedication
came with a price, however. Brown gave herself to only one
movement. It was only when the suffrage amendment was assured that she took up work against the forces of militarism.
Her complete dedication also colored her relationships with
others. She could not understand why many were so tepid in
their response. It was only when she was in her eighties
that she found among the members of the Woman's Party,
with their unswerving dedication and their radical tactics,
the kindred spirits she always longed for among her colleagues.

An understanding of Brown's indomitable will and un-
flagging constancy only becomes intelligible within the context
of her larger world view which was shaped by her religion.
Universalism provided Brown a vision of the future, a basis
for action, and an unrelenting commitment to the establishment of principle.

Brown's early corpus gives a hint of her interests and
how she applied her embryonic religious insight to reality.
In two rambling essays, "Female Character" and "Female
Education," which were written during her years in Yellow
Springs, Ohio, the young Brown confronted the issue of the

female condition. Although her subject matter was not religious, her remedy was.

What is female character, she asks? Literature, custom, and common parlance define woman as a drudge, a fool, an angel, an ornament. What is the truth of these designations? What most notably characterizes woman, Brown claims, is that she does not direct her life according to any fixed principle. She is a trifler. Butterfly-like, her aim is only to please. With no object to accomplish, she rests and enjoys the present and has no regard for the future.[35] Her education teaches her to be a coquette, and since she has no way to gain an honest livelihood, her only recourse is marriage. She passes from the protection of her father to that of her husband. Since she has not been taught a respect for truth, she becomes cunning and deceitful. Some learn submission to rules and clothes and become crippled and dwarfed, bigots who are mean, cowardly, and despicable. Some remain untamed and are wild, with no regard for others. Yet the natural qualities of woman--her perceptiveness, patience, endurance, enthusiasm--if directed by reason and given an object could become powerful instruments for good in the world. Brown confronts her sisters with the condition of their souls. You will be asked if you have used your talents, if you have lived for God and eternity or for man and time, she admonishes them. She urges women to recognize their true worth and claim responsibility for their destiny.

> Let them be no mere imitation, no tinsel, no gaudy glittering allusion to please for a moment but finally to disgust and weary the observer because wanting in true merit. If woman is an ornament, she is an ornament formed by the Almighty. Do not let falsehood and ignorance ruin his work but let it have room to expand and exhibit its full beauty.[36]

In these early essays Brown saw appropriate education as the means by which the condition of women could be improved.[37] The end of education, however, was always to bring the student to a commitment to principle and to work for the reform of society. This end was amply illustrated in an address Brown wrote in 1862 to her educated sisters in the Crescent Society, the female society at Antioch. In that address she argued that the issuance of the Emancipation Proclamation had established that the human soul is free and that this meant not only freedom for Negroes but for all men and women. She urged her sisters to claim that freedom for

themselves, to recognize their own dignity, to reject socie-
tally ordained images of women, and to go forth and do good
works in this world.[38]

For Brown it was the end of female education which
was of utmost importance. In an address on Margaret Fuller, the early nineteenth-century writer and transcendentalist,
Brown used her as an example of how an excellent education
without objective or goal could be perverting to the human
spirit. In Fuller's case, Brown argued, it produced an ego-
tistic and pedantic woman whose limitations were only
finally overcome when she dedicated herself to the goals of
the Italian Revolution. Although Fuller might be remembered
by many as one who sacrificed herself for her husband and
child, Brown argued that this did not truly mark her off from
other women who were similarly dedicated. What set Fuller
apart and gave cause to remember her was her search for
truth and her devotion to principle:

> The multitude are content with externals and acci-
> dents, they seek neither the hidden causes of events
> nor meaning of the objects about them. And how
> rare is that absolute truthfulness, that at the peril
> of individual comfort, ease or the favor of the
> world, will dare to be loyal to a principle when
> once it has been discovered.[39]

In Margaret Fuller's life Brown found such absolute truthfulness. "Loyalty to truth," she stated, "is to us the great
lesson [of] her life."[40]

For the young Olympia Brown the goal of women's education was to create a loyalty to truth. She urged such an
education as a means of improving women's condition. In
her own life she chose to live out that loyalty to truth in the
pulpit where she could speak directly to the establishment of
principle in the lives of her congregation. Throughout her
ministerial career she continued to maintain an interest in
the amelioration of women through their enfranchisement and
came finally to give herself totally to the cause of female
suffrage.

Olympia Brown's whole life can be seen as one lived
in loyalty to truth, in commitment to principle. Her ser-
mons and speeches reveal her understanding of principle and
its implications for life. The underlying assumption of
Brown's world view was the acceptance of a God of love and

justice who was manifested both in nature and the Bible, the creator God whose creation was orderly and filled with design, [41] the kind father who offered universal salvation to all creatures. [42]

For Brown the implications of these simple Universalist doctrines were far-reaching. Since universal salvation was ultimately ensured, religion came to be focused not on matters of personal salvation but on the uplift and service to humanity here and now. [43] Universalism was an appropriate religion for a busy age which had little time for theology. [44] It fostered progress and social reform and yet like all genuine religion it was not reducible to reform activity for "this alone cannot give life to the soul, it cannot refresh the fainting spirit and inspire our faith." [45] As genuine religion was more than reform activity, so the "true church" was beyond Universalism, or any denomination. The "true church" was made up of all those noble souls who loved God and humanity and were ready to do noble deeds; it was a church confined to no time or place. [46]

Brown's world view was eschatological. She believed that good would triumph over evil[47] and that the great victories of faith were not in battles but in the establishment of moral principle. [48] "Ours is the age of realization," she said, "the ideals which delighted former times will in our age become practical realities." [49] These ideals or principles were indestructible; they were established by God. The work of the true believer, or, as she said, "the true reformer," was to labor against all odds to realize them.

> The true reformer says to the world, you may destroy my body. You may stay my followers and yea you blot out this earth but you cannot destroy ... these truths. They are as indestructible as the great God who made them, whose will they express. [50]

Brown was well aware that a commitment to the establishment of principle meant suffering.

> She who would work for justice and right at the present day must be willing to encounter public odium. She must sometimes meet with the displeasure of friends and the contempt of enemies. The cause demands martyrs. They must be willing to give up other ties, other hopes, to labor for

the good of many. ⌐Feelings may be sacrificed, affection may be forgotten, principles must be defended. 51 ⌐

Yet the reward for such work was blessing, the love of truth
and virtue, and the pleasure of having done God's work. 52

For Brown one of the most important Christian principles was the inherent worth of each individual. 53 To be created human was to be created with freedom and equality. The
love of freedom was innate in God's creatures and the inherent drive toward self-protection was a manifestation of that
love. 54 To be creature was also to be equal to every other
creature in relation to the creator. The fatherhood of God
implied the equality of all mankind. It was the realization
of these twin principles of liberty and equality which Brown
believed was the work of her time.

> In our day the one great truth to which all are to
> be converted is that all mankind are born free and
> equal. This proposition is the basis of all modern
> reforms and as yet it sounds as strange and incom-
> prehensible to modern ears as did the precept, love
> your enemies, to the revengeful pharisees. 55

It was within the American Republic, the product of
countless experiments in past government, that the principles
of liberty and equality found their fullest realization. The
Republic was the vehicle through which the "democracy of
Christianity" was to be worked out. The doctrine of individual rights expressed in the Declaration of Independence was
rooted in the Christian belief that every human being was a
child of God and hence free and equal. 56 What confronted
America was the extension of this principle to its logical
conclusion: political equality between men and women. It
was to achieve that goal that Brown gave more than fifty
years of her life. Her dedication to the female franchise
was so complete that she argued that all those who claimed
to be good citizens and Christians necessarily would support
the enfranchisement of women.

> I was probably considered very narrow to make
> one's appreciation of another depend upon her judg-
> ment on a single subject, but when we remember
> what woman's suffrage means, that it involves the
> whole principle of democratic government and the
> doctrine of justice taught in the Golden Rule, we

> see that anyone who is wrong on these subjects
> could not be a very loyal citizen of our republic
> nor a good Christian. [57]

It is within the context of Brown's Universalist world view that her commitment to the female franchise and her disgruntlement with those who opposed it must be understood. Hers was an unbending loyalty to truth, a total dedication to living out her Universalist beliefs in the fatherhood of God, the brotherhood of man, and the liberty and equality of all people. In retrospect one can see that her life was of a piece. Her early concern for the degraded condition of women, her career as a minister, her dedication to the cause of female suffrage, and finally her commitment to curbing militarism all spoke of her loyalty to truth. It was such loyalty which prodded her to action and gave her a vision for solace when her commitment could easily have flagged. Her life manifests the fruitfulness of religious insight in providing the goals and ideals for reform in American history and stands as a confirmation of her hope that she "who works in harmony with justice is immortal."[58]

NOTES

1. Although Antoinette Brown was ordained in 1853 by the Congregational Church of South Butler, N.Y., her ordination did not meet the requirements of the Congregational denomination. Olympia Brown was ordained ten years later by the full authority of the Universalist Church. Hence, she was the first denominationally ordained female minister in the United States.

2. Olympia Brown, Autobiography, edited and completed by Gwendolyn B. Willis. Published in The Annual Journal of the Universalist Historical Society, Vol. IV, 1963, pp. 14-18.

3. Ibid., p. 18.

4. Ibid., p. 26.

5. Ibid., pp. 24, 26.

6. An interesting letter from Ebenezer Fisher, president of the Canton School of Theology, announces her acceptance to the school but indicates that Fisher would not encour-

age her to pursue a career in ministry. Letter from Ebenezer Fisher to Olympia Brown, June 21, 1861, Ser. III,
Folder 127, Olympia Brown Papers, Schlesinger Library on
the History of Women, Radcliffe College, Cambridge, Ma.
(Hereafter cited as OBP.)

7.   Catherine F. Hitchings, in her entry on Olympia
Brown in Universalist and Unitarian Women Ministers published as Journal of the Universalist Historical Society, Vol.
X, 1975, clarifies the circumstances of Brown's ordination.
According to research done by Ralph N. Schmidt, Brown was
ordained in June 1863 by the St. Lawrence Association of
Universalists in Malone, N.Y. This is substantiated by both
a letter from John Lee to Olympia Brown dated April 27,
1881, and by the Minute Book of the St. Lawrence Association of Universalists.

8.   Henry Blackwell to Olympia Brown, June 12,
1867, Ser. III, Folder 128, OBP.

9.   Letter from Olympia Brown to Susan B. Anthony,
March 16, 1882, in History of Woman Suffrage, edited by E.
C. Stanton, S. B. Anthony, and Matilda Gage (Rochester,
N.Y.: Susan B. Anthony, 1882), Vol. II, pp. 259-61.

10.   Formation of the New England Woman Suffrage
Association, TS, Ser. II, Folder 47, OBP.

11.   Brown, Autobiography, p. 38.

12.   Ibid., p. 40. Brown's papers reveal almost
nothing of her relationship with her husband. Their marriage
in no way seemed to restrict her work. Following the lead
of Lucy Stone, she continued to use her own name throughout her married life. In 1878, Willis agreed to follow his
wife to Racine, Wisconsin. Brown's daughter, Gwendolyn B.
Willis, in an epilogue to her mother's autobiography, indicates that John Willis was always "most sympathetic with my
mother's interests and enterprises." Autobiography, p. 66.

13.   Brown, Autobiography, p. 62.

14.   United States Citizenship, Address Before the
Government Congress, World's Exposition, Chicago, Il., August 9, 1893. Printed, Ser. II, Folder 29, OBP.

15.   Address on Woman Suffrage, MS, Ser. II, Folder
19, OBP.

16.   United States Citizenship, loc. cit.

17.   Crime and the Remedy, Address delivered before the Parliament of Religions at the Hall of Columbus Art Institute, Chicago, Il., Sept. 22, 1893, Printed, Ser. II, Folder 29, OBP.

18.   Address on Woman Suffrage, loc. cit.   See as well, Why the Church Should Demand the Ballot for Women, Printed, Ser. II, Folder 49, OBP.

19.   Woman's Suffrage.   Address Delivered at the Rockford Fair, Rockford, Il., Aug. 29, 1888.   Printed, Ser. II, Folder 29, OBP.

20.   United States Citizenship, loc. cit.

21.   Ibid.

22.   Address on Woman Suffrage, loc. cit.

23.   Gordian Knot, MS., Ser. IV, Folder 153, OBP.

24.   Olympia Brown, "Reminiscences of a Pioneer," Suffragist (Sept. 1920), p. 214.

25.   Olympia Brown, Acquaintances, Old and New among Reformers (Milwaukee: S. E. Tate Printing Co., 1911), p. 92.

26.   Call to the Final Meeting of the Federal Suffrage Association, to be held on January 29, 1921, TS, Ser. IV, Folder 153, OBP.

27.   To the Members of the Wisconsin Woman's Suffrage Association Assembled in Annual Convention, TS, Ser. II, Folder 32, OBP.

28.   History of Woman Suffrage.   Lectures delivered at Suffrage School held in Madison, Wisconsin, June 18-24, 1914.   TS, Ser. II, Folder 33, OBP.

29.   Brown, Acquaintances, p. 105.

30.   Brown, "Reminiscences of a Pioneer," p. 214.

31.   President Wilson's Appeal, TS, Ser. II, Folder 35, OBP.   Printed in Nation, April 16, 1917.

32.   Brown, "Reminiscences of a Pioneer," p. 214.

33.   History of Woman Suffrage, loc. cit.

34.   Permanent Peace, TS, Ser. II, Folder 36, OBP.

35.   Lead Us Not into Temptation, MS, Ser. II, Folder 89, OBP.

36.   Female Character, MS, Ser. II, Folder 21, OBP.

37.   Female Education, MS, Ser. II, Folder 38, OBP.

38.   Address to the Crescent Society, MS, Ser. II, Folder 23, OBP.

39.   Margaret Fuller, MS, Ser. II, Folder 50, OBP.

40.   Ibid.

41.   For I Pass By and Behold Your Devotions, MS, Ser. II, Folder 109, OBP.

42.   Behold I Bring You Tidings of Great Joy, MS, Ser. II, Folder 56, OBP.

43.   Crime and the Remedy, loc. cit.

44.   Olympia Brown, "Occasional Sermon," Presented before the Connecticut State Convention of Universalists, held in New Haven, Ct., Sept. 4, 1872.   Reprinted in Gospel Banner, Augusta, Me., Sept. 28, 1872, p. 1.   Ser. II, Folder 26, OBP.

45.   Who Shall Render to Every Man According to His Deeds, MS, Ser. II, Folder 73, OBP.

46.   For As We Have Many Members in One Body, MS, Ser. II, Folder 60, OBP.

47.   Olympia Brown, "We Have No Right to Die," Star in the West, Cincinnati, Ohio, Sept. 6, 1877, p. 1. Ser. II, Folder 27, OBP.

48.   Faith or the Old Reformers and the New, MS, Ser. II, Folder 43, OBP.

49. Moses Went Up from the Plains of Moab, MS, Ser. II, Folder 53, OBP.

50. Faith or the Old Reformers and the New, loc. cit.

51. Scholar Today, MS, Ser. II, Folder 42, OBP.

52. Faith or the Old Reformers and the New, loc. cit.

53. Speech. "Report of the Convention for Organization." Edited by Matilda Gage. Woman's National Liberal Union. (Syracuse, N.Y.: Masters and Stone, 1890), p. 54.

54. History of Woman Suffrage, loc. cit.

55. Faith or the Old Reformers and the New, loc. cit.

56. United States Citizenship, loc. cit.

57. Brown, Acquaintances, p. 51.

58. Gwendolyn Willis claims that this was her mother's favorite quote (Autobiography, p. 76). It is inscribed on a memorial tablet to Olympia Brown in the Memorial Universalist Church in Washington, D.C.

SUFFRAGE AND RELIGIOUS PRINCIPLE:
SPEECHES AND WRITINGS OF OLYMPIA BROWN

It is with the intent of illustrating Olympia Brown's underlying
religious vision that this selection from her voluminous Papers has been made.   Her corpus, which reveals the public
but not the private woman, consists of hundreds of entries,
most of which are in manuscript (ms.) form, some in typescript;
some have been privately printed, others are copies of published materials.   Many of these entries were drafts only
and were not intended for publication.   Editorial changes are
minimal, although punctuation, capitalization, and spelling
have been silently corrected.   Where changes or deletions
in the original were necessary, this has been indicated in
the text.

Education is our great duty in this life. Education, in its
broadest sense--physical, mental and moral--is the work
which is going on from childhood to old age; from the cradle
to the grave we are always learning. The first thing we do
after drawing breath is to learn life; and learn is an old
motto but a true one. Education makes us, gives us our
position in society, as Emerson said of manners, it marries
us and we marry it. Wealth and position are of no avail if
we have not that culture which gives us control of the powers
nature has implanted within us. In our day people are beginning to realize the importance of this subject; they are
beginning to learn that in a free country like our own everybody must be educated and even idiots in this day are taught.
The blind are taught, and something of reason is given to the
insane by proper training. By training, the dumb find tongues
and the deaf ears, the poor brutes are elevated into a kind of
companionship with man through their training. Even plants
learn to grow in particular directions and the vine will climb
up by the cottage door and shade the window and afford a
resting place for birds if only it is trained a little at first.
But when everything learns, when education is the watchword,
why is poor woman still spending her time on trifles? Why
are the eye and the fingers still the only recipients of the
advantages of culture? Long ago woman learned the alphabet; why does she not go farther? Does not the law of progress hold good when applied to woman? Has she reached the
highest round of her ladder by learning the alphabet? It cannot be! Then why has she stopped in her course with all her
imperfections, her feminine frivolities and her petty follies?
Someone will tell us she has advanced and will proceed at
length to compare her position with that of women in a savage
state, will tell us that barbarous nations made her a slave
but that now in these Christian days her servitude is light-
ened, that she is no longer the drudge but the ornament of
society; but it is questionable which position is most enviable
since as the ornament she is deprived of that discipline by
which her powers are to be strengthened and increased. For

21

the last hundred years female character has not been improving. Our mothers of the Revolution were better women than
any we have now. When we see effects we must look for
causes. If the women of today are feeble and inefficient and
trifling there must be a cause for this and we must look for
that cause chiefly in female education since human character
is so moulded and fashioned by that agent. We must seek a
remedy for this in a new system. Let us look for a moment
at the course of female education pursued.

The little girl is hardly out of her cradle before she
is a lady; she knows it and her mother knows it. She is ex-
horted on all occasions to act like a lady, hence it is rare
to see a little [girl] who is content to be herself but on the
contrary [girls] are generally trying certain coquetish graces
which they have observed in those older than themselves, not,
it is to be regretted, through any feeling of deference for
these older persons but rather through a sense of their own
consequence. The growing girl is for the most part deprived
of that exercise which her muscles demand to make them develop in their full vigor. The dignity and consequence of her
young ladyship forbids the free pure air which the good God
has prepared for her. She cannot run and jump and feel that
she is free but the first lesson she learns is of care. Propriety like a grim monster haunts her every step, drives
away every glad thought, checks every burst of childish merriment, frowns on her from all corners, imprisons her in
close rooms, makes her sit upright on hard stiff chairs, fills
her little lungs with impure air when she ought to be gathering strength of body and soul in communion with Nature.

By and by come the schooldays and in all the girl's
life there is perhaps no time when she approximates so nearly
to freedom and happiness as during those school days. Many
[a] one in the pride of womanhood, in the vigor of middle
life, has looked back with delight to the time when she played
by spy or ball on the green before the schoolhouse and Mamma,
none the wiser. There she laid the foundation for the little
health and strength she had. There she ran and shouted to
her companions with a boisterous glee forbidden before and
all unknown since. What if the teacher did frown grimly and
set the gaunt, haggard old ghost of propriety ... scowling at
her through the long forenoons? What if the little pale faced
girl in the corner who always smiled but never got her lesson did turn away in contempt and call her a romp? Nature
would have its way. A little while and the fresh young blood
that ran rushing through her veins for a moment defied the

world and broke the iron bonds of custom; but how dearly
was this liberty bought! What a price must she pay for the
bone and muscle gained on the playground? Here she first
did what she knew Mamma could never approve. Here she
first learned the lessons of secrecy and here she unconsciously
but surely laid the foundation for a life full of deceit. Here
while she enjoyed her first freedom and drank her first fill
of pure air insidiously was planted the germ of a worm which
should canker and beckon her soul forever. Long after, as
she dreamed of those days, she might never think of tracing
back years of sorrow and mental anguish to the first time
she played ball in study hours and kept it secret from Mother;
but there it was. The first deceit! It is like opening the
flood gates which shut out the sea, once started who could
say where it would end? It rushes on until in mad fury it
sweeps away all the old landmarks, all the corners where
goodness and virtue made a home, and finally it leaves the
heart a blank desert.

Beware young woman how you allow yourself to open
this door to wickedness even for a moment. But the freedom
of schooldays dearly as it is bought cannot last. It is but
for a moment that the poor girl is suffered to be herself.
The iron bands of custom are broken only to close around
her the tighter ere long her limbs are fettered and her whole
system wearied by those heavy long clothes. Oh! The
weary days when you first learn the lesson of submission
and obedience to dry goods, when crinoline reigns triumphant and the poor lady must regulate its every movement....
No martyr at the stake suffers more keenly or endures suffering more proudly than the young lady sustaining the honors
of the first long dress. Pity that this heroic martyrdom
could not be borne in a nobler cause. But though the foundation for a life of sickness and disease has been laid, though
a circle has been drawn around her which says thus far shalt
thou go and no farther, though her limbs have been as it
were literally hooped in, though the seeds of secrecy and
deceit have been planted in her young heart, there would still
be hope, were this all, but the worst is yet to come. She
is not yet finished. She has not yet attended the young ladies boarding school and on some fine morning she goes with
Papa and all her bag and baggage to this seat of refinement
and taste where one learns how not to do it more effectually
than was ever done in Dickens court of chancery. And being
fully presented to the antiquated matron, her life and liberties
are made over to that very respectable personage, to have
and to hold for the period of one year with particular directions

that she should have no communications with any young gentle-
man, although had it not been for this very direction the idea
would never have dawned upon her mind.

And now begins such a series of lessons in falsehood
and deceit that one must indeed possess more than mortal
purity to escape uncontaminated.   Rules upon rules, long
lists of rules are crowded into her mind.   She is called upon
to enter a report upon all manner of petty trifles.   At every
turn there is a rule to be broken and a report to be made,
upon the judicious wording of which depends the pleasure or
displeasure of her teacher.   Could there be invented a better
system for rendering one careless in respect to her word and
regardless of the importance of truth?   Impossible.   Our female seminaries are ruining the moral character of the young
women of this country.   The teachers are usually superficial
and frivolous and the time is taken up with insignificant details which instead of rendering the student considerate in respect to small things, serves only to harden the heart and to
dwarf and belittle the intellect.   All individuality is destroyed
through this conformity to needless rules.   Goodness and industry degenerate into slavish obedience which is in itself
contemptible.   You have rules to eat by and rules to sleep
by, rules to breathe by and rules to pray by.   Where then
can the ingenuity or individuality of the student be exercised
except in deceiving teachers in regard to these very rules,
and here is precisely where it is exercised.   Perhaps it is
not exaggerating to say that two thirds of all the young ladies
in any given female seminary are in the daily habit of deceiving and imposing upon their teachers.   And it is only because human nature is so much more prone to good than it
is to evil that some few good and true women emanate from
these institutions.   We can have no better argument against
total depravity than that in spite of all the machinery of the
young ladies boarding school, in spite of the two or three
years training in deception, not withstanding all the lessons
of frivolity and folly taught there, there is still something of
goodness and truth in woman.

Most young ladies before they graduate from these institutions get what is vulgarly called religion but which in its
practical workings is most unlike the religion of Jesus, that
is, they spend a week in tears, converse affectingly or at
least affectedly with the minister, and have a private and
touching interview with the teacher after which everything
goes on as before except that the young lady becomes more
vain and arrogant and has less of charity for her companions

than before. Those attending these schools may be divided
into two classes. The first are those who having some physical vigor possess a certain degree of animal life, a kind of
quickness of intellect and readiness of speech. They are
usually denominated, the wild girls. Give these wild girls
an opportunity for mental development, something to look forward to, open to them an honorable field of labor, awaken in
them a praise worthy ambition and above all let them have
plenty to do and they become talented and noble women. But
instead of this they are sent to the female seminary not [to]
acquire knowledge but to be tamed. They begin to cheat.
They impose upon their teachers and upon their mothers at
home. They grow lawless, have no regard for the rights or
property [of] others, and by the time they leave the institution are prepared for almost any wickedness. The second
class are the so called good girls. You may know them by
their pale faces and shrinking figures. They have been good
too long. They have been pattern young ladies ever since
they could stand alone and their constitutions have suffered
thereby. They are wanting physical strength and vigor and
could they rest and lay aside care and run in the fields and
grow strong for a year or two and then acquire some thorough knowledge, they might become valuable members of society, intelligent and energetic and ready to live a life filled
with good works. But instead of that they go to the female
seminary to be polished. They spend two or three years
there in servile obedience to rule, mechanically pursuing the
same monotonous routine at the end of which they come out
crippled and dwarfed in mind as well as in body, intolerant,
bigoted, mean, and cowardly.

    This specimen is not so positively wicked as her com-
panion, the wild girl, because she has the requisite courage
and physical energy of two characters, the one so dangerous
and the other so despicable. It is impossible to say which
is to be preferred, yet nearly all the members of our female
seminary belong to one class or the other. Fortunately, however, life at boarding schools like all other earthly things is
transient and must have an end. At last our young lady goes
forth thoroughly accomplished, according to the popular phra-
seology. She plays a little on the piano, has learned a few
scientific terms, she knows little or nothing of mathematics
and less if possible of the classics; not [with]standing her
father's parting injunction she has learned to conjugate the
verb amo in several languages though of the real meaning of
the word she knows as little as the languages in which she
gabbles it. In her wardrobe and expenditures she rivals the

notable lady who had nothing to wear.   Could you witness the
unmeaning and objectless course of her life you would think
her the heroine of nothing to do.   And should you chance to
listen to the silly prating which she styles conversation, you
would certainly suppose her the original of nothing to say.
What now is to be done with the girl with all these acquire-
ments?   During all this time the idea of depending upon herself for support has never entered her mind.   She has not,
like her brothers, been choosing for herself some honorable
and lucrative employment by which she should render herself
independent and perchance do something for others.   Every
thought of this kind has been studiously kept from her.   She
has been taught to believe it beneath the dignity of the family
that she should have any particular calling.   To earn money
for her own support she regards as degrading, and yet her
father is unable to meet her expenditures.   There is for her
but one resource, she must marry; it matters little who or
what, black, brown or grey if he is only presentable in society and has a good supply of the needful.   The verb amo
in any of its shades of meaning is very little thought of in
this connection.   No art is left untried.   The powers of paint
and perfumery are tested on all occasions, drooping eyelids,
modest blushes and pensive attitudes are made to do their
share.   She affects literature, and unable to wade through
anything solid devotes her time to Chip Edgeworth novels;
imagines herself in a trying position; supposes father, mother, sister or aunt, as the case may be, to be a cruel persecutor; becomes an invalid; laughs, cries and has hysterics
but revives on the entrance of her favored suitor.   Finally
she gives herself body and soul to the man with the money,
although her ignorance, inexperience and youth render her
wholly unfit to assume the care of the household.   Mamma
sheds a few natural tears, feels that it was for her daughter's happiness and on the whole is glad to see her well settled.   She was so troublesome.   Papa thinks she is well disposed of.   He has done his duty much to his own satisfaction
and realizes sensibly that a great tax is taken from his heart
as well as his purse.   Her sisters, if she has any, are glad
she is gone because they well know there will be the better
chance for them.   So ends the history of the education of the
young lady of today.   Can any one consider for a moment the
different influences brought to bear upon her mind from infancy and then wonder that female character presents so complicated a problem?   It is no wonder we have backbiting and
lying and dissension among us when women are brought up to
these things; women who are to give the first direction to the
minds of our statesmen and our authors, they who are to be

the constant companions and perpetual partners of our greatest men. These who play so great a part in the whole organization of our social life are educated to nothing but weakness. They have weak bodies, weaker heads, and weaker hearts. Do not wonder that we hear of divorce cases, cases of theft and cases of murder, when you remember that one half of our population are educated to nothing but folly and deception. Do not start back with horrors and amazement that the city of Cincinnati contains over a thousand prostitutes. Remember that these women had an aimless, objectionless education, that no hope was presented to them in youth save that of pleasing men. They were not taught to enter into business and to earn a livelihood for themselves. Do not be surprised that when the only hope they ever had has been blighted and care and want comes they turn to the only resort left them. Do not blame these poor women but look to your own firesides and if you have daughters, educate them to be independent, to have an object in life. Educate them so that they may have within their reach the means of gaining an honest livelihood. Educate them in time to be good and true instead of to please ... and you need have [no] fear for them. It is society that makes prostitutes, the systems of female education pursued now are well calculated to make them. It has been estimated that New York City contains over 8 thousand of these wretched creatures and that the proportion is about the same in the other cities of our country and from the investigations made, it has been ascertained that the greater part of these are nearly uneducated in the more solid branches, that most of them have adopted this kind of life not willingly through any evil inclination but that they have been driven to it through absolute starvation and want, that in many cases they have for months struggled against it with all the energy of despair and that at last they only yielded to the natural instinct for self preservation. An author in the Dial traces this monstrous evil back to a want of lucrative female employment. Let us go one step farther and say it is the want of female education. Women are not prepared for lucrative employments, they have not been taught to engage in business, to sell goods, to keep books, to set type, to engrave and a hundred other things which might have saved them from starvation or perdition. They have not been taught to depend on themselves and when the hour of need comes they know not where to turn or how to ward off destruction.

Parents, can you think of these beings reduced to degradation and crime without a shudder, without feeling the cold chill of fear that some of the young women now growing up around you without aim or object in life, without strength or independence will one day meet the same fate? Do not suppose your friends are different from others; human nature is the same everywhere. Perhaps your family is above want and you feel that you have enough of this world's goods. But if wealth is all your dependence, frail indeed is your support. How many families have you seen suddenly hurled from affluence to the most abject poverty and how do you know but some unlooked for revolution of fortune may reduce you also to want? If you would give your daughters something which will be unfailing support, something which will place them above want and above danger, which will serve them faithfully in the hour of need, give them knowledge, knowledge of themselves, ... knowledge of life as it is and above all knowledge of some honorable and lucrative business. Educate them in all that serves to cultivate and enlarge the mind, in all that makes the faculties stronger or more skillful, not that they may become great or renowned but that they may be independent.

Do not leave them to marry for a home or to depend upon matrimony as a means of support. Husbands are liable to die, to be sick, to be poor, to be intemperate and [there are] a hundred other chances in which a woman will wish to depend upon herself.

But you say, there are no employments open to women. Let women be educated for the employments and they will open themselves. Six months or a year devoted to the study of short-hand will prepare one for a reporter and how easy a thing for a young woman of reliable character and skill in the business to become connected with some of our best newspapers and make her fortune. A few months at one [of] the commercial colleges and a little natural aptness enables one to gain a respectable livelihood at bookkeeping. How easily might a young woman learn dentistry or the jeweler's trade or cutting in marble, all good employments and eminently suited to women.

The occupations are not wanting, the natural fitness in woman is not wanting but the requisite education to prepare woman for these places is all that is wanting. Educate women and as children let them be children. Let them run and romp and grow strong and vigorous, full of animal life, full of courage and strength. Let them try the capacities of their lungs and you will save them from the consumption afterwards. Some women have weak voices because they have

never, since they cried in their mothers arms, exercised
their lungs by a long, loud shout.   Let the merriment of
childhood and the buoyancy of youth have its way.   Give them
liberty and let their peculiarities of taste and disposition appear.   Women are not all alike, they are not all made to
cook and sew.   Let them follow the tendencies which nature
has given to guide them.   Some knowledge of mathematics
and of science, a little of language is necessary in whatever
department, the more of those the better.   It is better for
the cook or the sewing girl to be well informed, to understand the histories of nations, the constitution and laws of
her own country, our own literature and the literature of
other peoples.   There is no danger of having too much or
too thorough knowledge if it only be made practical and useful.   A full college course is a good foundation upon which
to build an elevated, moral and intellectual character.   It
matters not what the occupation: it will be serviceable alike
to the authoress and the seamstress, to the lawyer and the
shoe black.   A few colleges are free alike to all the youth
of our country.   There young women may gain that knowledge
which will be to their souls as light and air to external nature.   Herein, studying with their brothers, they feel an interest in the subjects and a zeal in the pursuit of knowledge
never realized in schools designed for ladies only.   Let all
young ladies who can, go to these and first securing a good
basis for their [further] intellectual culture, choose for themselves such professions or employments as they feel to be
most congenial.   Some have objected to the joint education
of the sexes on the ground that it affords an opportunity for
those heartless flirtations which are at once injurious to mind
and morals, but in the experiments that have been tried thus
far it has proved quite otherwise.   The time and attention
are given to other subjects, science and literature crowd out
petty trifling; flirtations are mostly originated as a sort of
an exercise for feminine talent for the want of some other
theater of action.   There is always danger when a human being has nothing to do.   The mind is naturally active and if it
is not engaged in something good, the chances are that it will
employ itself about something evil.   A well managed flirtation
is the only scope society gives for the intellectual activity of
woman.   But give her employment, give her something worthy
as an object of thought and an objectless flirtation is out of
the question.   What woman interested in science, tracing the
laws written by the Almighty on tablets of stone all over this
fair earth of ours, unraveling the mysteries lurking in the
simplest chemical combination or following the great mind
of Newton in his demonstrations, could turn aside to flatter

a weak human being in order to deceive?   By another class
it is objected that intellectual culture unsexes woman, that it
makes her manlike.   Think ye that by taking thought ye can
add one cubit to your stature?   Do you suppose that by any
process we can add one quality to mind or heart the germ of
which was not implanted by an almighty Father?   As well
might you insist that we could create a world if we could
create one new faculty as firmness, comparison, or causality
we might create souls to order.   All that education can do
is to develop and improve the qualities already existing, to
arouse the latent energies and to make the mind grow by exercise.   How absurd then to talk of unsexing woman by education.   It is because she possesses intellectual faculties,
because she has reason and reflection God-given, that it is
her duty to cultivate these powers.   If a woman has a natural
predilection for science or art, for metaphysics or mathematics, it is as if a voice spoke from Heaven and called her
to the work.   She commits a sin in closing her ears to this
voice and in confining herself to the needle or the cooking.
Not that we would have woman loose any thing of grace or
beauty or elegance which she now possesses but that all those
qualities will be heightened and increased by mental culture;
not that she should loose one charm but that she should gain
many.   They tell us that the development of the intellect is
antagonistic to the tender feelings, that the heart is more important than the head as if benevolence and kindness were at
war with reason and reflection.   Is God less good because
all wise?   Is he less merciful and loving because omnipotent
and omnipresent, because he knows and understands all the
perfect character, comprehends the full development of the
intellectual, moral, and sensational natures?   There is no
war between heart and head, they are allies firmly united,
each rejoicing in the prosperity of the other.   Knowledge
serves only to guide, to direct and to strengthen the affections.   But just here we are confronted with the old hack-
neyed selfish question.   If women are educated and engaged
in business, who will cook our dinners for us?   The domestic circle, sweet home, a cottage on the hill side where love
reigns and a host of visions of a similar nature arise [up] at
once to the frightened mind of the sentimentalist.   But if all
this sentiment, if the delight of the dear domestic circle is
to be based on female ignorance, how frail is its foundation.
Sooner or late the light of knowledge must shine in upon every
human heart and if the sweetness of home is to be marred
thereby, let it go.   Let us regard it but as a delight attendant upon the infantile days of the race.   But what reason have
we to suppose that the permanency of the home circle, the

sweetness of domestic life or the wholesomeness of dinners
is to be lessened by female education? Would this not tend
rather to bind the home circle more firmly together? By
rendering the home influence not merely emotional, not merely
an influence exerted through the medium of the feelings but
one dependent for its weight upon the intellect and reason as
well, does it not become more potent? Is there not a stronger tie binding heart to heart when two can reason together on
subjects interesting to both, when the husband finds in the
wife a companion who understands and appreciates those subjects that are engaging his attention? Divorce cases would
be less common if women were more congenial companions to
men of intellect and learning. The author of Titcomb's letters tells us that men must spend their evenings abroad, that
they must go down town to clubs and other places in order to
come in contact with other minds, as if the society of their
wives afforded no intellectual refreshment. It is a sad pass
for society to come to when men are obligated to go to clubs,
to visit barrooms or to lounge in post offices through the long
winter evenings in search of that intellectual companionship
which they cannot find at home. If they had wives of cultivated minds, wives of nice literary taste or of scientific
knowledge, where could they better discuss the [merits] of
the last new work in the threatened dissolution of the Union
than at their own firesides? The old myth that intellectual
women make poor wives is based on the grossest animalism.
He whose idea of home is of nothing except of a place where
he eats, sleeps and is monarch of all he surveys will perhaps fear the influence of education in his domestic domain.
It is the cowardice of the tyrant that keeps subjects in ignorance. But he who seeks in a home the companionship of
loved one, the elevation of his tastes, the cultivation of his
mind, the advice and counsel of one who sympathizes with his
every thought, such [a] one will say, let science and learning
find a home upon my hearth stone, let the light of knowledge
illumine my family circle and let my wife be a sharer in all
that should engage the attention of one made in the image of
his maker. Home is rendered not less interesting by the
union of head as well as heart, dinners not less wholesome
because prepared by one of intelligence. If a woman is a
cook her bread is none the worse for her knowledge of philosophy or chemistry but if she is no cook, which a great
many are not, as is well attested by the ill prepared food we
find in so many houses, why there are plenty of those who
are and who are suffering for want of work. Our cities are
full of women starving for want of the means of earning a
little pittance to keep them alive. Why not employ these and

let the woman who [has] neither task nor talent for cooking
do something more profitable? If she has children, her time
and strength will of necessity be devoted to their education.
She cannot do everything and each one should do the most
ennobling thing of which she is capable. But perhaps some
sentimental young man in broken tones will murmur that when
he marries he wants to feel that his coffee and his pancakes
are prepared by the same hand that smoothes his pillow and
arranges his arm chair by the fireside. He can eat sour-
bread and it will taste sweet if he knows it was mixed by the
loved fingers, but to eat food mixed by a hired Irish girl
would destroy domestic bliss and dispel the happiness of home.
As well might the sentimental young lady exclaim with tears
starting to her eyes, a delicate blush suffusing her cheek,
how can I bake the potatoes which have been planted and dug
and picked up by a hired menial? What delight there would
be in boiling [cabbage] which had been set out by that hand?
It would be pleasure to live in a poor leaky house if it had
been built by the one I loved. Luckily however this exacting
class is rapidly diminishing: they are melting away before
the advance of civilization. Those who expect one woman to
do everything, who always ask for their dinner whenever the
subject of woman's position in society is referred to, are
comparatively few. But setting aside these other considerations, women should cultivate their minds as a source of happiness. Many an hour is spent in a peevish melancholy, when
it might have been employed in storing the mind with beautiful
thought. The woman who depends upon the society of others
for happiness must learn the anguish of disappointment and
the weariness of ennui. She who has resources within herself, who enjoys the companionship of the good and great of
all ages through their works, has an unfailing source of happiness. The loss of relatives, the neglect of friends, cannot
destroy her peace of mind. Many mothers, anxious for the
happiness and well being of their daughters, are fearful that
unfortunate affairs of the heart should rob them of their peace.
But give them food for thought of another character and there
is no fear. There is no better antidote for the memories of
blighted affections than the preface to Livy or the differential
calculus. Severe study in any form is a sure remedy for low
spirits, melancholy, hysterics and all such ladylike afflictions.

Through study and mental discipline the character of
woman is to be changed from feebleness and inefficiency to
strength, bravery and truth. Woman has a soul to save; her
position in the world to come will not be estimated by the
moral elevation of her husband or her father in that land

where there is neither marrying or giving in marriage.   She must stand upon her own merits.   The question put to her will be what is the condition of your own soul?   How much have you in your character that is Godlike?   How much has your spirit gained in strength, in truth, in purity by the discipline of life?   It will matter little then whether her husband was rich or poor, learned or unlearned.   The question is how have you improved the talent committed to your keeping?   And the women of today will reply--we gave our souls in charge to our husbands; we have neither strengthened nor improved the powers that were given us; we have not been laboring to make ourselves pure and upright.   Unholy before God, we have been endeavoring to please and conciliate men. Sisters, are you willing, when the trials of life are over, to make up your account in this way?   Are you willing to allow evil customs and superficial education and false ideas to sap the foundations of your moral character?   Are you willing to surrender your soul to the shackles and corruptions which society throws around you?   Are you willing to meet your God with the reply, I lived not for you but for men, not for eternity but for time?   Methinks I see you shrink from this answer.   Then turn your energies and your talents towards the subject of female education because it is the only sure way of reforming and elevating female character.   It is perchance the work of years to revolutionize the prevailing systems of female education and to lead women to be guided by principle and to have a motive in their actions.   It may be the work of generations; the cause, must from its nature, progress slowly for though the spirit is willing the flesh is very weak.   Long time must we labor even to effect a change in woman's physical education, still longer before we can reach the mental and moral.   But the greatest works are accomplished slowly, slowly are the most sublime ideas developed, slowly the giant forces of nature work their wonderous revolutions, slowly.   Slowly God unfolds his mysterious laws to man, slowly scientific truth is evolved and recognized, slowly civilized nations arise from the rude chaos of barbarous tribes, slowly will the true, strong, noble woman come forth from this melee of folly, deception and vacillation, slowly will the true principles of female education come to be understood and adopted, but because slowly, not less surely; not less surely are mountains leveled and valleys upheaved because centuries are involved in the process; not less surely does God reveal himself to man because his great truths require ages for their demonstration.   Even now must the work begin.   Let us see in every ignorant and outcast woman a being possessing capacities which being developed

would make her almost divine; let us see in her an object
calling upon us for light, asking us for education. Says the
Dial in speaking of the outcast and degraded one, she shall
be to us a being of awful [grandeur], an immortal child of
the omnipotent, bearing his image, living by his protection
through the tatters and rags of earthly defilement; we pierce
to Heaven descended, soul burning within her flame, clouded
indeed, but imperishable as God. Let it be ours to dispel
the clouds which envelop her intellect and bid the clear sun
of knowledge shine in upon her hemmed faculties, quickening
them to new life, awakening a new energy in the universe of
her mind. As Goethe said when he died, Let the light enter,
let the light enter the soul of woman awakening it and revealing it in all its power and its symmetry. For a little while
it has seemed that she had paused in her onward course but
the great law of progress and improvement still holds; onward toward perfection is the cry. There is no time to
pause. It is the darkest just before the dawn; even now
while darkness seems to enshroud the soul of womankind
we hear the distant sounds which bid us hope, for the light
of morning advancing, already the physiologist has spoken a
word for fresh air and outdoor exercise to make woman
strong and vigorous; already the gentle tones of a female
preacher are guiding her sisters toward truth. "This way,"
she says, "sisters," but the sisters have no strength to follow her pure teaching; they lack mental discipline; they want
education. But the morning is breaking, women who have
been slumbering must be up and doing; They must secure the
advantages of culture through their own effort. The future
of woman depends upon herself, it depends upon the young
women whose characters may yet be moulded into symmetry
and disciplined to strength. They must begin it at home, in
their own hearts must the change be wrought; into their own
minds must the knowledge enter which shall make them wise
and good. Through their own patient exertion must they
reach that firmness and stability of character which can
alone enable them to fulfill well their duty, here and when
life is ended to return to God who gave his own with usury.

The poets represent woman as an angel. Philosophers describe her as a fool, and the usages of common life make
her a drudge. How shall we resolve these three contradictory views into one true picture? How make a unity of this
trinity for doubtless the poet and the philosopher have each
a grain of truth in [their] theory. And the usages of common life must always be founded upon some fitness of things
like the two knights in our old story books who quarreled
about the color of the shield. They see different sides of
the same object and receive different impressions all true
perhaps and yet when placed side by side with other truths
these views become so modified, so changed in their whole
aspect that they are no longer the same. The drudge, when
viewed through a halo of idealities, when considered in respect to her patient endurance, her faithful industry, her
long suffering yet without complaint, may attain to the beauty
of the angel; while the angel deprived of its wings, clad in
homespun and invested with those emblems of office, the
broom and the dishcloth, becomes nothing more than the
drudge. A few irregular pieces of glass placed in a frame
and seen through a prism arrange themselves into various
beautiful figures assuming the appearance of pyramids and
castles; while pyramids and castles seen through the mists
of ages are but a heap of ruins strewed about the earth.
The child all unacquainted with life, who can scarcely remember his own name, is transformed into the wise man by
time and cultivation and the wisest man is but a fool when
compared with that mind which contemplates the whole universe in an instant. Thus truth is seen only in parts, we
can only approximate towards the entire by bringing together
these different views. The different rays of light with their
varied colors must be united to form the clear white light,
which is so grateful to the eyes which reveals every object
in nature. Thus in considering human character we must
observe partially at first, and by uniting and combining those
various observations we must form a true estimate. It is
an old fable that when the world was created and all that is

35

there in the different animals [was] endowed, each with a peculiar and ruling quality of mind, thus the lion was made
ferocious, the hare timid, the fox cunning, and the dog sa-
gacious but when the maker of all came to man, the various
passions and emotions had been exhausted and man was made
of the remnants of all, and therefore possesses to some extent the characteristics of all.   How complicated a problem
then becomes the study of man's mind, nothing less than the
study of the shreds, the odd three-cornered pieces of all
imaginable thoughts, feelings and volitions.   But the mind
of woman presents an enigma yet more perplexing.   Essentially the same, yet differing in appearance it presents only
a different arrangement of the same rags and remnants, a
different permutation of the same quantities, or an atrophic
state of the same body.   And our perplexity is increased
since we must penetrate the obscurations of paint and po-
matum.   We must add something here and subtract something there to allow for inaccuracies of observation caused
by looking through the halo of the formalities and requisi-
tions of society.   Hence the false and absurd views which
have been from time to time put forth, hence the mistakes
which the world is always making in respect to her qualifications, education and sphere of action.   The character of
woman has indeed been treated of from the earliest times,
but for the most part in a light and superficial manner as
if it mattered little and as if no human being was to be influenced for good or evil by these treatises.   The moralists
rarely picture to us a really true and noble woman; their
ideal women are generally vain and foolish or sometimes
they make them overflowing with benevolence, mild as a
summer's morning, gentle as the evening zephyr, but they
are insipid and vacant in mind such as we could not enjoy
a half hour's conversation with.   Dickens, that great revealer
of character, such an observer of peculiarities that he seems
to be picturing out an old acquaintance all the time, has failed
completely in his heroines.   What is there to admire or imitate in such a character as Little Dorrit, at best a half-
starved, fear-stricken child, who did the best she could under the circumstances.   In Esther Summerson, we have the
same style of character, nothing superior, nothing noble,
simply a careful prudent woman but on the whole one better
fitted for a servant than for any other position.   All his good
women partake of this nature.   They are abject, shrinking
creatures without knowledge or positive excellence, unless a
kind of instinctive benevolence pass for excellence, character[s] far more interesting as [children] than as ... actor[s] in
the great drama of life yet such is undoubtedly his highest ideal

of woman. [Currer] Bell in Jane Eyre has approximated more
nearly to a true delineation of female character and it is natural that woman should best portray her own emotions and
springs of action.   But even Jane Eyre is at last made the
victim of passion and the animal seems finally to triumph
over the intellectual and moral.   It is not a true picture of
life, as it is neither an ideal which we should wish to imitate.   Now and then, indeed an author presents a character
which for a time attains to something of the dignity of the
noble-souled intellectual woman but for the most part it has
not been sustained through the whole work when it has been
even attempted, and generally it has been found easier, more
pleasing to the vulgar taste and more in keeping with other
literature, to represent her as a benevolent puppet.   But fiction, to be well received must have some foundation in fact.
Characters, to interest the readers must be descriptions of
nature; they must be pictures of those we see around us;
hence these poor caricatures do indeed represent one side
of female character.   The course of education laid down for
her, the ideas instilled into her mind are of so dwarfing and
belittling a nature that it is not strange we find her with a
feeble sickly mind, rarely indeed do we picture a woman
who seems to have arrived at full intellectual maturity.
Dickens does well to choose for his heroines those who by
circumstances have been cramped and turned aside from their
natural course, those born and bred in prisons far from the
light of day or in some wretched hovel where human nature
can scarcely be expected to stand forth.   In all the dignity
and grandeur which becomes a being, animated by a spark
of Divine, it is but an exaggerated picture of woman's education and life.   Authors depend more upon personal experience than upon imagination and they must describe the things
they see around them even if they are imperfect and distorted.
If I should describe the potato bud as a long, white stem with
only a tuft of leaves at one extremity, no botanist, no observer of nature, would recognize the thrifty deep green plant
of the gardens.   Yet if you go into our cellars in the Spring
you may see what that plant may become when cut off from
light and air.   So the human mind if cut off from those ac-
tivities which are its chief means of growth, if fed on sickly
sentimentalities, if shut in by petty conventionalities becomes
weak and inefficient, incapable of anything really great or
noble and from this feeble, starved specimen authors have
derived their descriptions and their theories of the female
mind; but history, more truthful in its delineations points out
now and then one who has given evidence of the life that was
in her; here a Zenobia rules the East with a mighty power,

Miriam rejoices with Moses in his triumphant march out of
Egypt and joins with him in leading on this follower to the
promised land, and in modern times a Madame De Stael has
shown us the power of woman's influence when her intellect
is suffered to develop itself in its normal manner.   Even the
haughty Napoleon trembled before the weight of [De Staël's]
pen.   Tyranny and oppression, fearing for their own existence, drove her from France, and Liberty found in her a
friend and defender.   Napoleon, the greatest man of modern
time, he who subdued the world and made nations tremble,
owed most of his strength to the controlling [influence] of a
wife whom circumstances and custom had not been reduced to a
mere fashion plate and whose mind had attained to something
like its natural strength.   England has boasted queens, powerful in government, wise and prudent in the management of
affairs and in our own land; science has found an able in-
vestigator, theology an earnest expositor in woman.   But
these examples are rare, they are only here and there, just
to show us what we might become and to open to us in part
the mental and moral greatness for which Providence designed
us.   The mass of women are terribly unlike these brilliant
examples; the intellectual and moral standard which women
present to themselves is exceedingly low.   It is the common
cant of society that woman's intellect is small, that she cannot reason well, that she cannot grasp great questions but
that her instinctive nature is her chief ornament.   And we
hear much about her angelic nature, her moral purity, etc.,
but, my friend, look around among your acquaintances and
point out one whom you think to possess this ethereal nature.
Is it Mrs. White the widow across the way?   She is certainly
a kind and benevolent woman but you remember very well that
when you bought milk [from] her she made it half water, and
that when she sold butter she cheated in weight.   She cannot
surely possess that elevated moral nature which you declare
to be the ornament of female character.   Then there is Mrs.
Barton, the school teacher of your village.   True she has
some intellectual culture and can scarcely be called an example on your side but as her education has been very limited she may possibly correspond to your representation of
woman.   She is mild and patient, works all day in the school-
room for a mere pittance, but are you willing to admit that
she is the angelic being you describe?   No, you call to mind
that when you were one of the school board she falsified in
several particulars with regard to her school, that she de-
ceived you about her qualifications.   She is no angel, she is
only a weak woman and yet she is better than most of the
women in your village, because she is stronger and her mind

is more disciplined than theirs. These generalities do very
well to talk about, there are no better epithets for sound,
than angelic nature, Christian virtue, guiding Star, Sister of
Charity, etc. But where is there one, except perhaps her
whom you may have adopted as your Dulcinea. Where is the
one to whom you are willing to grant these qualities? There
is no such one. Positive virtue cannot exist without knowledge or strength. How can one discriminate between right
and wrong or firmly resist temptation who has no mental
stamina? The child is well disposed, good natured and quiet
but how little a thing disturbs him and rouses his evil tem-
per. How slight a gewgaw will please his fancy and attract
his attention from the lesson you are trying to teach him.
The sheep likes the food you give him, his instincts draw
him towards it but how innocent and trifling a thing will
serve to frighten him away from this of which he is so fond.
A natural inclination towards virtue, an instinctive love of
right is of very little value if there is no knowledge to guide
and no mental discipline to aid in maintaining truth against
opposition. That women have neglected to cultivate their in-
tellects, that they have failed in most cases to store their
minds with useful knowledge is most true, but it is the moral
feebleness and inefficiency which grows out of this that we
feel most keenly. Women do not direct their lives according to any fixed principle. They do not act in accordance
with any settled purpose. They do not propose to themselves
any particular object in life, but heedless of the great world
full of duties, neglectful of those powers given them to direct
their course, they live on, guided by the caprices and whims
of others. Their thoughts and opinions [are] controlled by
those of whom they obtain their daily support and they only
[are] mindful of what they shall eat or what they shall drink
or wherewithal they shall be clothed. The women of this
age are asking for rights, some of them are demanding the
elective franchise, but at every turn we are met by the assertion that women are not prepared to vote, that they are
too ignorant and too frivolous to be entrusted with so powerful an agent. It was urged the other day to me that not one
woman in ten had ever read the Constitution of the United
States. That beyond a vague notion that Columbus discovered
America and Washington was the father of his country, they
are entirely ignorant of our history, that their interest in
politics is confined to looking at a torchlight procession or
in presenting a flag to some political club. How true these
assertions are let every woman judge from her own observations, but certain it is that women are wanting in true mental culture and in real moral worth. The young lady who

visited Niagara Falls and was pleased because she said it was
so nice, is a type of a large proportion of our young women.
They are mere butterflies sporting in the sunshine; their only
aim is to please; whatever you say no matter how absurd the
proposition it can but meet with their approving smile.   They
are as anxious to agree with one another as the two Dutch-
men who meeting on a fine summer's morning said one to
the other, "What you tink die wetter will be?"   His companion paused to consider so profound a question.   He looked
North, South, East and West, smoked his pipe and replied,
"Well I tink die wetter will be wat you tink de wetter will
be."   To which his companion replied after due consideration, "I tink de wetter will be just wat you tink de wetter
will be"; after some time spent in smoking, Dutchman no. 2
responded, "I tink so too."

      To contend for a principle, to maintain any opinion by
argument, is considered as beyond the sphere of womanhood.
And unable to express any sentiment really their own, our
modern [ladies] stand entirely noncommittal on neutral ground
on all subjects and so far from being interested in the welfare of the country they for the most part agree with the lady
who feared to represent one of the States at a fourth of July
celebration lest people should suppose she was patriotic.
They waste their time and energies on trifles, a pet dog or
cat, a bird or a rabbit, assumes a wonderful importance in
the eyes of these exceedingly refined damsels.   The success
of Liberty, the victory of Truth, the Emancipation of three
million slaves are as nothing compared with some of these
little fancies.   The following clipped from one of the newspapers of the day well illustrates their style of correspond-
ence, as well as their kind of education.   It seems to have
been addressed by some graceful maiden with drooping eyelids in a moment of despair to her darling Augustus.   "To
Augustus.   Return to your darling, devoted petite.   She won't
be naughty anymore and will send Ponto away if he snaps at
you again at the usual place at seven.   Don't fail if you would
not make your petite miserable.   Au revoir," says the paper.
If Augustus can hold out after such an appeal then his heart
must be harder than the Sphinx's.   The offer of the darling,
devoted petite to sacrifice even Ponto, the name probably of
her other pet poodle, upon the altar of affection is a proof
of devotion which it does one good to contemplate in a girl
of the present day.   Therefore we hope that Augustus will be
at the usual place wherever that is, at seven, to a minute,
that the devoted Petite may not be made miserable.   A little
of French, just enough to say au revoir and to call herself a

petite, enough of rhetoric to write a billet-doux, enough of
logic to enunciate the following propositions: Augustus must
be pleased; the sacrifice of the poodle is necessary to please
Augustus; therefore the poodle must be sacrificed, enough of
sentiment to sigh for an absent lover. This makes up the
mental acquisition of how many of our young ladies? To understand the use of money, to know how to acquire and to
appropriate it, this is something entirely beyond their prov-
ince. They graciously subsist upon the bounties of Papa until he is either out of pocket or out of patience and then they
are in market as the saying goes. That is, they are ready
to lavish great wealth of affection upon the man who has the
longest purse, and as Papa's pocket and patience are never
a constant quantity but are always subject to variations, it
follows naturally that they are constantly upon the lookout for
some owner of Bank Stocks who is ready to make a large in-
vestment in woman's love. The following story has undoubtedly been seen by many and well illustrates the blunders into
which a lady is sometimes betrayed by having this idea in
matrimony too constantly before the mind. But it is not
merely as an intellectual weakness that we regard these
things, if [it] were only this, if the only result was to keep
her in a state differing little from that of servitude, if it
were only that she is deprived of the power of exerting any
influence for good; it were a small thing, but we must consider the effect of this limited intellectual training upon the
moral nature. Where we have causes we must expect effects. If an individual is idle and vacant in mind it is reasonable to look for gossiping. If the attention is confined to
subjects of little moment and what is said upon these subjects
is considered of no consequence, we can but look for a recklessness of truth. If one's support and standing in society
is made to depend upon pleasing merely, we may look for
cunning and deception. If the mind is trained to yield and
to be submissive on all occasions we must expect to yield
to and flatter the wrong as well as the right. These causes
and these effects we see every day around us. We find
women universally as wanting in morals as in mind. Her
deficiency of moral principle instead of being contemplated
with sorrow as a serious evil in society, is made a subject
of joke. It is regarded as a matter undisputed, as a rather
laughable, agreeable fact than otherwise, that women are
nearly all gossips. The old woman's tea party where half
a dozen middle aged ladies meet, take tea and discuss their
neighbors affairs, talk over the new bonnet of Mrs. C. and
the awful expenditure of the Misses D., has become a part
of our literature. There is scarcely a schoolboy but has

attempted some description of it and novelists unnumbered
have made capital of this feminine entertainment and it is
truly a lamentable fact that whole villages have been set in
commotion and the happiness and reputation of families uncounted been endangered by the imprudent and improper conversation at these same tea parties.   But it is not merely
that other peoples' affairs are discussed here, but gossiping
leads to lying and through this it happens that the word of
most women is not reliable.   I blush while I acknowledge
that in my dealings with women, I have almost invariably
found them false.   They are false to each other and to themselves.   Long used to regard what they say as of little importance, the subjects on which they talk being of a trifling
nature, they accustom themselves to trifling with trifles until there is nothing upon which they can be serious and true.
The most solemn compacts are made only to be broken and
they even boast of the light and easy way in which they can
put aside a promise; treachery to their friends seems but
pastime.   Long ago, Samson was betrayed by a woman and
our modern intellectual Samsons are too often mistaken in
those whom they keep in ignorance yet whose instinctive virtue they declare to be the controlling influence of their lives.
Long versed in efforts to please, dissimulation becomes one
of the feminine graces; it is practised from girlhood until it
becomes a second nature and it is deemed unladylike to
speak the truth.   A frank and an honest manner is considered evidence of idle breeding and the best etiquette nowa-
days consists in having a word and a smile for everybody,
even wrong doing must be smiled upon.   It would be unladylike to frown.   And young women will meet cordially in society young men of acknowledged intemperate habits and those
whom they know to be guilty of the grossest offences, and
not only this, but they will agree with whatever false and absurd opinion may chance to be expressed by these.   Instead
of bravely contending against the evils existing in society,
attempting to reform the erring, to put down intemperance,
to correct unjust and illiberal opinions, they give countenance
to all these things.   They encourage drinking by flattering
the drunkard, they increase ignorance by scoffing at reforms
and by smiling complacently upon the vicious, they lend a
helping hand to crime.   Not long ago I heard a temperance
lecturer charge the ruin of a fine talented young man upon
young ladies of my own village.   This young man, gifted by
nature, possessing all those advantages of social position and
intellectual worth which would render him an agreeable addi-
tion to any society, was tempted to drink while calling upon
these young ladies; since then he has been going down, down

to the very dregs of society. What, my friends, do you
think is the moral condition of young women who will urge
a young man to drink? Perchance he had a natural tending
toward that fault, a long time had he been struggling with all
the energy that was in him to overcome that evil which beset
him on all sides; thus far he had been successful, friends
had been watching anxiously for his reform and hope had already portrayed a long and happy future for him. But here
were two young ladies whom he esteemed, young ladies whose
opinion he cherished most highly, who laughed at his scruples
as being unworthy a man and fit only for boys, who offered
him the glass with their own hands, nay even pressed it upon
him until at last he yielded and with that glass he fell? How
do these young ladies stand before God? Where was that
moral purity which they tell us is woman's chief ornament
which is to take the place of knowledge and of independence?
I know another one who had, under circumstances the most
trying, resolved upon reform, one who had promised reform
with all the solemnity which the horrors of his approaching
destiny inspired. He went away into a remote place where
he deemed he should be free from temptation and where, de-
voting himself to study, he should be enabled to forget his
old companions and his old faults. But even here in this
retired place, in this spot of seeming safety he was enticed
and led on to drink by a woman. What must have been the
condition of that woman's moral nature? Where is the delicate moral sense of the woman who spends money in ruthless
extravagance, lavishing untold sums upon her own fine clothes
when there are so many suffering human beings around her,
when she might every day meet young ladies whom with a little of her superfluity she could relieve from want and prepare
to gain an honest livelihood for themselves. Where is the
human feeling of her who can look around upon the want and
suffering of poor women and then oppose the opening of other
and more lucrative employments to them? And yet, so
strange is the female character that she who attempts to
open any new field of labor for women or better the condition in any way meets the most severe opposition from her
own sex. I presented the petition asking for woman the right
to control her own property and time to a lady in middle life.
I asked her to sign it. "No," said she, "I won't sign it. I
haven't got any property myself and I don't ever expect to
have." Where was that instinctive goodness, that virtue without knowledge that we hear attributed to woman? The woman
was ignorant, every faculty of her mind was dwarfed and
therefore she was wanting in benevolence. There cannot be
positive excellence without intellectual development; the moral

is based upon the intellectual, they are not antagonists, they
grow together and strengthen each other. Most people do as
well as they know how. It is because of wrong education, of
imperfect knowledge, of one sided culture, that people are
extravagant and selfish and false and deceitful and vicious.
I have spoken of a few of the prominent faults prevailing
among women. I have done so only with the hope that being
seen that [they] might be the more easily avoided, for woman
was made for better things, the last best, the crowning work
in the world's creation, was not designed to be this feeble
abject being. Providence had in store for her a great work
in the economy of Nature. She was endowed with those qualities which should have fitted her to fulfill her mission well,
amid this wreck of intellect, this ruin of moral character,
you can see the traces of what might have been a noble being. There is a grain of truth in nearly all falsehood and
so in the common cant of society, false as it is, there is a
grain of truth. Women are not angels, they are not at present essentially pure and excellent. But they have within them
capabilities which being cultivated and brought out they would
become worthy of the higher calling which they have upon
Earth. Quick to perceive, patient in endurance, they possess the very qualities which under the proper culture might
fit them for a high position in intellect and in morals and
enable them really and truly to exert that influence which
fancy has so long attributed to them. The female mind possesses a certain fineness which eminently adapts it to the
discussion of nice questions and to making delicate discrimina-
tions. It is a favorable omen for the future that the work on
intuitive morals, the best of its kind at the present day, was
written by a lady. There is also in woman a certain enthusiasm which could it be directed and controlled by principle
would be one of the greatest agents for reforming and civiliz-
ing the world. Those very qualities which now serve only to
make her ridiculous in the eyes of the world and to render
her influence pernicious in society and destructive of the peace
and happiness of neighborhoods, when guided and directed by
the light of reason, when furnished with a worthy object,
would become one of the most powerful instruments for good.
In the field of science her patient endurance and her quickness to perceive relations would become the means of bringing new truth to the world and of discovering relations already existing between those truths already discovered. The
character of woman has not yet been brought out and the
world has failed to recognize the germs of goodness and of
greatness which have so many years been suffered to lie dor-
mant, which die out for want of activity and that knowledge

which is the food the soul feeds on and without which it
dwindles away and dies.

But illumine these fainting souls with a few rays of
knowledge, arouse these sluggish minds with hope, the hope
of doing and of being something of themselves, take these
poor hearts and heads out of the stifled atmosphere of the
parlor and the kitchen and give them an airing, open to them
the great world full of life and light, tell them to do their
duty as conscience dictates the impossible to none but God,
and mark the change.   Woman is no longer a selfish, frivolous creature with some benevolent impulses but with no
principle or strength.   She becomes earnest in her endeavor,
firm in purpose seeking out the right of every question, independent in opinion and in action, no longer a burden upon
husband or father, no longer a tax upon society, a clog upon
whomever she is connected with, a creature to be supported
at the public expense, but an inventor, a scientific discover-
er, an educator, a manufacturer, a worker, and withall a
woman, always graceful, always modest and prudent possessing all those qualities which now render the character of
woman loveable yet strong in her own conscious integrity,
firm because acting with knowledge and reason, looking to
God not to men for support and approval, proud in possessing the attributes of an elevated human being.   Not one class
of individuals alone would be made better and happier by this
change, but everywhere throughout the inhabited globe we
should see the results of new light and liberty.   No member
of society can be enlightened and elevated without benefiting
and improving others.   Society takes its color from the individuals that compose it, even the humblest menial cannot
be improved without producing a due influence upon those
about him.   If the waiter at a hotel is gentlemanly and polite,
if he exhibits all those qualities of mind and person which
serve to adorn humanity, you are the gainer, your character
is made better even though you should never meet him but
once in your journeyings.   Those who are brought in daily
contact with him feel that they are associating, not merely
with a servant, but with one of Nature's noblemen and they
must deal with him kindly, justly and honorable.   If your
seamstress is an individual of mind, if she has thought and
read and knows what life is, it is for your advantage.   The
benefit is not hers merely, it belongs to every one in your
town.   You feel more of respect, you have no longer to deal
with a poor piece of clay which plies the needle at your
command but you are brought in contact with another mind.
Perchance your soul is enkindled by a spark from hers, you

see qualities in her which are worthy of imitation. She has
ideas which find an answering chord in your own heart. She
is capable of culture, is improved by her intercourse with
you and you also find your soul-life strengthened by communion with one who, though her lot has been cast far differently from yours, is still one of God's creatures. Nor
is this all. Every other laborer in your vicinity, seeing the
strong purpose of her life is led to work with more of vigor
and of hope for they know that though toilers they are yet
human beings and in mental and moral worth may equal any
in the land. Thus whatever the theory of woman's mission,
to whatever sphere society may consign her, her character
and qualifications cannot fail to affect all. Certain it is that
society has never yet contrived to do without women and perhaps it never will, if so, how much better that she should be
made the instrument of good than that so much human ingenuity, so much of the labor of brave and noble [women]
should be expended in the vain attempt to gratify caprices
which spring from an undisciplined and vacant mind.

Society is elevated in elevating its drudges and if
woman is to be, as she so often is, a drudge, how much
better that she should be an intelligent and responsible one.
Not a mere drudge but one whose beauty of mind and heart
will elevate the work she does. Men are known by the things
they admire. They may be judged by the ornaments of their
households since these ornaments in time become mirrored
in their own souls. If women are designed like pictures or
rocking chairs only to make life pleasant and homes cheerful, if they are, as some maintain, mere ornamental pieces
to preside at tea tables and receive attention in parlors, still
more is it important that these ornaments be genuine. Let
them be no mere imitation, no tinsel, no gaudy glittering al-
lusion to please for a moment but finally to disgust and weary
the observer because wanting in true merit. If woman is an
ornament, she is an ornament formed by the Almighty. Do
not let falsehood and ignorance ruin his work but let it have
room to expand and exhibit its full beauty. Do not crowd it
into close stifled rooms but give it fresh air, let the glad
sunshine play over it. Place it in the best light, use it as
well as you do your pictures and other ornaments. If you
had a picture which required a particular kind of setting you
would feel that you did yourself and the artist an injustice in
keeping it in a narrow and awkward frame, letting the dust
collect upon it or hiding it in the dark. Here you have an
ornament which demands intellectual cultivation to bring it
out. It wants room and liberty to appear in its best light,

it requires a framework of mathematics and metaphysics, of
science, and philosophy; it should be hung all around with
truth and knowledge.   Will you refuse to provide these sur-
roundings when you can gain so much by doing so?

If woman's an ornament, let her be a masterpiece
such as God only could fashion.   The good workman is known
by his instruments; his tools are always the best, he cannot
work with a dull and rusty iron.   Some tell us woman is
nothing in herself, that she derives her power from man,
that only through him can she be instrumental for good.   If
so let her be a good tool.   It is for the honor of mankind.
Let her be no mean instrument but with a mind all furnished
and glowing with knowledge, with a heart made pure and clean
by the discipline of this world, let her be an instrument
worthy of the best of workmen.   In fine weather you con-
fine woman to the kitchen or the parlor whether she be an
instrument or an ornament, whether a fool, a drudge or an
angel.   The good of society and the well-being of the race
demands for her the fullest mental and moral development.
And to you who claim for woman the rights and responsibilities of a human being, I would say lay a good foundation for
your claims in making yourselves strong, true and earnest.
Sisters, if you would fulfill well your mission either in private family circle or in the world of business, either as
wives and mothers, or as members of society, labor faithfully to elevate your minds and to store them with useful
knowledge.   Prepare yourselves well for the work before
you.   Be faithful, be earnest, in short be ye perfect even
as your Father in Heaven is perfect.

To the Graduating Members of the Crescent
Society, Antioch College

Dear Sisters,

How gladly would I rejoice with you tonight in all that
makes you happy!

At the distance of more than a thousand miles I imagine myself in the midst of your meeting. I think that I see
your faces and hear your voices, and my soul exults in the
faithfulness and energy of the daughters of Antioch. As one
by one you take your places upon the stand I seem to listen
to your words and I say, truly I have formed a virtuous
woman for, "strength and honor are her clothing"; "she
openeth her mouth with wisdom and her tongue is the law
of kindness." But while I take delight in the noble women
who have arrayed themselves in strength and wisdom in the
halls of the Crescent society, a shade of sorrow mingles
with my rejoicing because I think of the trials which await
you in life. The times in which we live are frought with
much that is mournful, much that is hopeful. Society seems
to be passing through one of those mighty convulsions which
always mark the advent of some new order of things; the
shaking off of old fetters, the putting on of new liberty.
Pregnant as these changes are with good to society, it is
a solemn thing to live at such a time. What a fearful thing
would it be to be present at one of those giant upheavals
which change the face of nature and usher in a new geologi-
cal era! Not less fearful is it to live when the clash of
arms and the fury of contending hosts make old customs
totter and fall and prepare the way for a new epoch in history. It was such a time as this when the Jewish people
saw with horror the Roman legions surround their city and
witnessed the destruction of their beloved temple and of all
around which their hopes centered. It is a fearful thing to
witness any of God's judgments upon the wicked, for no hu-

48

man power can turn away the consequences of wrongdoing.
It is a momentous thing to live now; while a nation is suffering under the vengeance of a Just God, and while all over
this country Rachel is mourning for her children; when the
throng of human beings as it passes to and fro is breathless
and trembling with anxiety and expectation; when the shock of
conflicting views resounds through our land, startling the
happy family seated around their peaceful fireside and sum-
moning forth the father or the brother, the best beloved from
that circle and calls him away to do battle under the burning
heat of a southern sun. At such a time as this, when so
many good men are shedding their blood for the cause of
liberty and setting examples which will live through all time,
who can afford to be trifling and frivolous, to waste time in
fashionable follies, or to look with slothful indifference upon
the great interests at stake! Surely educated women cannot.
You and I are not permitted to join the ranks in the battle
and to fight against the enemies of the country, but have we
therefore nothing to do in deciding the important issues of this
contest! Do we live in vain at this time of revolution and
reformation? There is something more in this struggle than
a trial of strength, something more even than the question of
liberty or slavery for the black man. It is a trial of the
strength of republican principles in this country. The question is whether all human beings are entitled to life, liberty
and the pursuit of happiness. In its decision there is need of
great moral force among the people. Here at the North there
is need that liberal ideas, both religious and political, be
more firmly established in the hearts of all; that every community be made so strong in its attachment to freedom that
no power can shake it in its determination to sustain truth
and liberty. This work is given into the hands of those who
may not fall fighting by the side of their brothers in a noble
cause. The work of confirming, preserving and strengthening
liberal ideas, this general carnage has been committed to a
great extent to women. It is no mean task; it calls for zeal
and effort: it requires talent and energy. It is the work of
heroes and the bravest of heroes is the non-combatant.
Among the mighty men who surrounded Napoleon, there was
no braver one than Baron ... the surgeon in chief of
the Grand Army. It was his to heal the wounds and to bind
the broken limbs caused by the ravages of war. Catholic in
his feelings, he knew no distinction between friend and foe,
but a sufferer whether Russian, Austrian, English or French
he was ready to do this work, often periling his own life to
save others. He won the admiration of all the daring men
whom the daring spirit of Napoleon called forth. It was of

him that Napoleon said in his will, "He is the most virtuous
man I have ever known." And when the history of our own
day shall be written, by the side of the bravest generals in
the contest will stand that of Mrs. Ricketts, a non-combatant
hero. In after ages women will be animated to noble deeds
by the story of how she gave herself up and became a volun-
tary prisoner in the hands of the barbarous enemy that she
might watch over and provide for the wants of a wounded husband who had been borne away a prisoner at Bull Run. Such
examples as these show us that the truest bravery is shown
not in destroying the species but in preserving it. Not many
women are called to minister to the wants of men suffering
upon the battlefield. It is not the duty of many to go, like
Mrs. Ricketts to the camp of Gen. Johnston, and offer themselves as victims for the good of others, but the same courage, the same self-sacrificing spirit, the same determination
of purpose devoted to promoting the cause of liberty at home,
might work a revolution without striking a blow. Had the
women of this country, North and South, been like Mrs.
Ricketts, slavery and warfare [would have] been done away
long ago. Courage and determination are as necessary in
preserving virtue and independence in peace as in gaining a
victory in war. My sister, you come upon the stage of action at the most eventful period which has yet appeared in
the history of civilization. The work of emancipation has
begun, not alone in the District of Columbia, not alone in
the seceding states, but all over this republic has been begun the emancipation of the soul from its bondage to super-
stition, from its subjection to false customs and human dic-
tation. The proclamation declaring the human soul free has
gone forth not from General Hunter or Fremont but from a
higher than human court. It is not in the power of the President of the United States to revoke or to call it back. It is
to be carried into effect not by an advancing army leaving
blood and ruin in its train but by the enlightened moral sense
of the people of these northern states. They are the chosen
ones to whom God has committed his love of liberty, liberty,
not for Negroes alone, freedom not merely for the souls of
white men, but emancipation for all men and women.

        Liberty requires some degree of vigor of thought and
action. It would be of little use for Gen. Hunter to proclaim
liberty to a slave who should not know enough to accept the
gift and use it, but who should crawl groveling at the feet of
a master declaring himself unable to be a man. It is of little use that God has given women understanding if that understanding is to bow in submission to every foolish custom which

happens to be foisted upon society.   It is in vain that he has
given her intellect and individuality if she has not the courage
to use them.   You to whom it has been given to enjoy the
advantages of education and of culture have a great work to
do in establishing the perfect law of liberty.   Much depends
upon your steadfastness and zeal.   If you are called to labor
as public teachers or in some useful department of business,
go bravely to the work and give to it a woman's energy and
earnestness.   If it is yours to be the center around which the
loving family circle gather with united hearts, be true to
yourself and to those who look to you for the principles which
shall go with them through life and whom it is yours to lead
into the fullness of intellectual freedom.   Do not be content
to be either an ornament or a drudge in your home but while
maintaining what is true to your own dignity and self-respect,
labor faithfully for those whose welfare it is your highest
pleasure to promote.   Be like the wife of John Bunyon, as
undaunted she stood in the Swan chamber before all the assembled dignity of England and addressing herself to Chief
Justice Hale demanded her husband's liberty again and again.
She was repulsed but she maintained her ground.   Time after
time she calmly replied to their statements, "My Lord, it is
false, " and when the question was put "Will your husband
leave off preaching?" with true heroism, though her husband's release hung upon her reply, she said, "My Lord,
my husband dares not leave off preaching as long as he can
speak. " Like this noble woman, have the courage to face
the highest in the land in a just cause, and the firmness to
maintain your rights before any tribunal.   Do not yield your
principles in religion, in politics or in social life to the
wishes of any.   Do not give them in exchange for honeyed
words of flattery.   Do not sell the soul's birthright for a
mess of pottage.   But whatever your lot, go forth to good
works, in the words of Lord Clarendon, "with a heart to
conceive, a head to contrive, a tongue to persuade and a
hand to execute. "

        I dare not trespass longer upon your time.   I would
that I could write out my whole heart to you but I only hope
that I may have said a word which may hereafter add encouragement in the moment of doubting or strength in the
hour of trial.   I feel that in the duties which lie before me
I shall have your sympathy and as far as practicable, your
cooperation.   I know that although distance may separate us
our spirits are united by ties which will not be sundered
either in this world or the world to come.   Similar objects
and similar views must serve as a bond which neither time

nor distance can sever. And wherever your duties may call
you be assured that the love of a sister Crescent will follow
you.

ON MARGARET FULLER
(ms., n.d.)

Dear Friends, Ladies of the club, our hostess has asked me
to say some things to you about Margaret Fuller. I have
never given a lecture upon the subject as she supposed when
she extended the invitation, although I once gave a brief account of her life at the social meeting of my church.

The events of her life have no doubt become familiar
to you by the studies and investigations of your previous
meetings and I think it best therefore this evening to follow
the train of thought suggested by our hostess when she asked
what characteristics of Margaret Fuller seemed to me now
admirable, most worthy of our emulation. In judging of her
character we need to remember that the position which women
occupy and the opportunity which the world offers them has
changed materially since Margaret Fuller's youth. She was
a forerunner rather than a representative of the true American womanhood. It was hers to go forward in the wilderness
crying, "prepare ye the way and make straight the paths for
a nobler womanhood which is to come after me in this free
America." Imagination suggests to us a more evenly balanced and grander character which she might have attained
had she been able with her wonderful gifts to avail herself
of the facilities for education which the present day affords.
If instead of gathering up the crumbs of learning of which
were permitted to fall from the rich man's table she had
been freely invited to the banquet of science, literature and
art, which our great institutions of learning offer, we should
have seen not a one-sided, egotistical, self-conscious pedant
but a large-souled, practical, devoted woman. For admire
Margaret Fuller as much as you may, all must admit that
her character was far from symmetrical and of a peculiar
and abnormal type which should little desire to [be] presented
as an example for imitation. That painful self-consciousness
which made her offensive to many upon first acquaintance was
not a mark of the well balanced mind so happily described by
Wordsworth:

The reason firm, the temperate will.
Endurance, foresight, strength and skill;
A perfect woman nobly planned
To warm, to comfort and command.

We pause with wonder but surely not with pleasure
when we read that just before her journey to Europe she says,
"I have met all the people worth knowing in America but have
met no intellect comparable to my own." Such egotism is a
blot upon any character however beautiful in other respects,
for humility is always a mark of real greatness. We in-
stinctively feel with the monk who had been summoned to
make a long journey to see a young woman reputed to possess peculiar and miraculous gifts and therefore supposed to
be an instrument in the hands of the Lord. Upon arriving
he investigated the case and finding her proud and imperious
and unwilling to perform common and homely tasks, he cried,
"Here is no miracle for here is no humility!" So where we
find insufferable egotism we are to feel here is no true greatness, for here is no conception or reverence for things higher
than one's own self. But in Margaret Fuller, these faults
were not faults of her nature but rather unfortunate results
of the peculiar conditions under which her education was received. At home by her father she had no opportunity to
bring her ability into comparison with other students leading
a similar life and pursuing similar studies. She felt herself
to be alone without sympathy or companionship and thus iso-
lated. She naturally felt there was in her nature something
peculiar and superior which gave to her the appearance of
egotism and contempt for others.

Such a nature as hers rebels against the restraints,
the narrow routine, the pettiness and superficiality of the old-
time ladies boarding school and seeks a freer atmosphere, a
larger liberty and a deeper hold of real knowledge. And feeling herself hampered, hemmed in, misunderstood, finds another support for her supposed [vice].

When women possessed of great intellectual vigour and
large attainments find no practical, congenial work of the
world in which to use their gifts, no worthy enterprise in
which to lose themselves, they are too often thrown back
upon themselves and dwelling in the ideal, they become vi-
sionaries; their views of persons and things unreal and unjust, and their judgement of the relations between themselves
and others perverted. Thus, in the case before us, Margaret's isolation, her studies and pursuits, the vast differ-

ence between her own education and that of the young women
about her, the limited scope for the use of her abilities which
they then afforded, all budded to induce in her that unrest,
that overweening self-consciousness and wonderful egotism
which made up the disagreeable elements of her character.
That these were results of education and circumstances rather
than essential qualities of her nature was shown by the great
change which came over her after she went abroad.   When
amid the excitements of the Italian revolution she found a
field for the exercise of her best powers, and when love had
touched her heart kindling there a Divine flame making her
forget herself for others, then we see no longer the self-
conceited, self-conscious pedant, but the disinterested philanthropist, the brave heroic woman, the devoted wife and mother
willing to live and labor for those she loved and choosing to
die with them rather than to live without them.   We are
charmed by this woman's devotion and courage, that in the
hour of shipwreck and peril [she] would calmly sit singing her
child to sleep that he might not suffer from the terror or confusion of the time and finally could die rather than seek safety at
the expense of the lives of those she loved.   But these are
qualities which she shares with a host of women of all ages.
The world has ever been enriched by woman's love; barbarous
times have been redeemed, savage society has been made
beautiful and common and homely scenes have been glorified
by wonderful instances of woman's devotion.   We may find
examples of these all around us, we entertain angels unawares and no one of you but can recall among your acquaintances those whose lives are a constant illustration of
the power of woman's love, to lose itself in the well-being
of others.   When then we seek for that quality in Margaret
Fuller which we should strive to imitate we look for something above and beyond the experiences of every day, something more than the wifely loyalty, the motherly devotion of
which every little hamlet furnishes notable examples.   We
seek something which shall be to us an inspiration, revealing the higher, the Divine nature which exists to some extent in all, but which shines forth preeminently in the great
leaders who from age to age have been the bearers of light
and truth, making the nations glad by their coming; the
saints, the prophets, the saviors of the race, lights shining
into the darkness and too often the darkness has comprehended them not.   Margaret Fuller was one [of] those inspired persons who are permitted to behold things not revealed to the ordinary observer and able to walk along a
pathway toward which common men and women may look
wonderingly but dare not approach.

And I find the characteristic which most distinguishes
her from others, which is most admirable and therefore most
worthy of our imitation, to be a nice discernment of and an
unswerving loyalty to principles.   The multitude are content
with externals and accidents, they seek neither the hidden
causes of events nor meaning of the objects about them.
And how rare is that absolute truthfulness that, at the peril
of individual comfort, ease or the favor [of] the world, will
dare to be loyal to a principle when once it has been discovered.

In these things Margaret Fuller was preeminent, not
alone above all the women, but most of the men of her day.
To her it was given to discern the life concealed behind the
outward form, to read as in an open book the hidden mysteries, and to reveal the principle which runs through and
governs events and which we call the Divine Law.   In her
summer on the Lakes, speaking of western life, she says,
"I trust by reverent faith to woo the right meaning of the
scene, perhaps foresee the law by which a new order, a
new poetry is to be evoked from this chaos."

And this she did in every place.   She wooed and won
the mighty meaning of every scene.   She sought and found
the law whereby a new order and a new poetry might be
evoked.   This is shown in her social life, in her association with the men and women about her.   With the penetra-
tion of the clairvoyant she searched the inmost thought, the
hidden motive and revealed it unsparingly.   Thus, she became a benefactor, a guide, a comforter to many; a warning, a terror to evil doers, says her biographer.   Margaret
saw in each of her friends the secret interior capability which
might become hereafter developed into some special beauty
or power.   By means of this penetrating, this prophetic insight, she gave each to himself, acted on each to draw out
his best nature, gave him an ideal out of which he could draw
strength and liberty hour by hour.   Her judgments took no
bribe from her sex or her sphere nor from custom nor tradition nor caprice.   She valued truth supremely both for herself and others and again she drew her companions to sur-
prising confessions.   She was the wedding guest to whom the
long pent up story must be told.   She extorted the secret of
life which cannot be told without setting heart and mind in a
glow....   This readiness to discern and declare the hidden
principle gives the key to her religious life.   In an age when
men were creed bound, seeking the letter of the law rather
than its spirit, following the traditions rather than the light

from heaven she sought the absolute truth, the light that lighteth every man that cometh into the world, and breaking away from the old tradition, she dared to be a transcendentalist.

Transcendentalism has been defined by Dr. Channing to be an assertion of the inalienable integrity of man, of the immanence of Divinity. In instinct it was the pilgrimage from the idolatrous world of creeds and rituals to the temple of the Living God in the soul. The maxims of the transcendentalist were trust, dare, and the infinite good is ready for your asking; seek and find. Leaving old formulas and rituals she came to the fountain of eternal truth. She smote the rock and the waters gushed forth at her bidding.

This same quality led to her judgements of the customs of society and her perception of the needed reform. She everywhere sought and found the law whereby a new order and a new poetry might be evoked. Hence, her readiness to perceive the wrongs done to woman, and at a time when the woman's rights reform was almost unheard of, to claim for women the right to enter any profession or business, to share in the rewards of the world and to bear in responsibilities equally with men. Justice between women and men and between man and woman; liberty and opportunity for all, was to her the Divine law whereby the new order and the new poetry were to be evoked from social chaos.

She saw clearly through all the sham and pretenses of society, the hampered life, the monotonous round, the weary discontent of many women. In her observations upon the West, beneath all the promise of growth and material wealth, she noted the weary plodding, [and] thankless toil of the women of the country. She saw the crushed hope, the stifled aspiration which makes so many women's lives sad. She said, "The life of woman must be outwardly a well intentioned, cheerful dissimulation of her real life."

She saw in all history how blindly women have received, unquestioning, the statements and the precepts of men, like the woman whom some travelers found living in a little lonely hut at the top of a barren mountain. She said she and her husband had lived there for forty years. They asked her why she chose so lonely and barren a spot. She didn't know, only it was the man's notion. So for many ages women have accepted loneliness and toil and servitude because it was the man's notion. And Margaret Fuller, looking behind the veil and beholding the unmasked deformity of the lives of many women cried grandly:

As to this living so entirely for men, I should think
when it was proposed to women they would feel at
least some spark of the old spirit of races allied
to our own.   If he is to be my bridegroom and
Lord cries Brunhilda, he must first be able to
pass through fire and water.   I will serve at the
banquet says the Walkgirl, but only [he] who in the
trial of deadly combat has shown himself a hero.
If women are to be bondmaids let it be to men
superior to women in fortitude, in aspiration, in
moral power, in refined sense of beauty.   You who
give yourselves to be supported or because one
must love something are they who make the lot of
the sex such that mothers are sad when daughters
are born.

As the Divine law, capable of bringing a new order
and a new poetry into woman's life, she recognized the principle of human rights, justice to all, and she claimed for
equality with men under the law and in the world of business
for she looked forward with prophetic vision to the time when
man and woman may regard one another as brother and sister, the equal pillars of one porch, the priests of one worship.

Loyalty to truth is to us the great lesson [of] her life.
She teaches us to find out the true thought, the right idea,
the hidden life.   And having found, to follow it to the end;
she bids us woo the mighty meaning of each scene and seek
the Divine law by which we may evoke a new order and a
new poetry.

In concluding my few remarks I can do no better, I
am sure, than to read her grand words at the time the an-
nexation of Texas was proposed with the expectation that it
would rivet more firmly the chains of the unslaved.

Her words to women seem like a grand rallying cry,
worthy a Napoleon at the head of his army.   They may serve
to stimulate us to a new loyalty in some of the great conflicts
between virtue and vice, temperance and intemperance, purity
and sensuality, conflicts in which men are powerless without
women's aid.

Mary hath chosen that good part which shall not be taken away from her.

There is in most people a tendency to overestimate the comparative importance of the work in which they happen to be engaged. Men are apt to look with contempt or pity upon those who are ignorant of the department of knowledge with which they are most acquainted and to regard other employments as less reputable than their own. So much is this the case that I have recently seen it stated that a company of miners accustomed to work underground refused a good employment because the work to be done was above ground. Although sadly needing the compensation for the work, they preferred to deny themselves and go without work to doing anything disreputable or beneath their dignity. It is this same spirit which gives rise to the hostility to the use of new inventions and improvements which is sometimes manifest; the same which is seen in the opposition which is made to everything new or untried.

It was with this spirit that Martha came to complain of her sister. Accustomed to seeing the women of that day engaged only in menial labor or in sports and amusements, she looked with suspicion and jealousy upon the serious studies and pursuits in which Mary took delight. In an unchristian, and in many respects a barbarous age, it had been considered the promise of women to serve; to do the menial labor, to carry the water and perform all manual labor. Both learning and religion were not considered to be within the reach of their powers. The culture of the soul, the development of the intellect formed no part of the education of the Jewish women ... and hence we may well suppose when Mary devoted herself to the study of the truths which Jesus taught, delighting in the great principles which were unfolding to her mind and dwelling upon the words of the Savoir, we may well suppose that the women of that time wondered and criticized, thinking it an evidence of folly and presumption and supposing

59

that she sought not so much to gain a higher and truer life
as to avoid the necessary duties and manifest destiny of
women.   Their feeling was the natural result of their ignorance and limited experience and the complaints of Martha
were but the expression of the feelings of a conscientious
faithful woman who knows nothing beyond her daily round of
labor and perceives no realities beyond the visible and the
natural.

But the reply of Christ rebukes such ignorance and
narrow, unjust judgement.   Mary hath chosen that good part
which shall not be taken from her.   This is the new gospel,
the glorious tidings, the golden promise for woman.   She had
chosen the truth of the Lord for her own.   She had shown
ability [to] comprehend great principles, to understand the
laws which govern the world.   She had manifested a desire
to enter into the realm of knowledge of spirituality and of
eternal life and this good choice was not denied her and hereafter she was to be no longer a servant merely.   She was to
be recognized as a human being, gifted with reason, with
spiritual perceptions, with ability to penetrate the mysteries
of nature, to comprehend science and to hold converse with
God.   This good part, he says, shall not be taken away from
her, no not in all the ages.   Wherever the name of Christ is
known or recognized, wherever the truths he taught hold sway
and society is governed by Christian principle, there the soul
of woman is to be recognized, her intellect cultivated and her
liberty secured.

Christianity opened a new life to woman.   It brought
to her the glad tidings of salvation from servitude, from ignorance.   And as a Christian civilization has advanced, her
position has been improved, her character elevated and her
sphere of labor extended.   The subject of the education of
young women is receiving considerable attention at the present day and the words of the text give sanction and encouragement to those who are urging a higher standard of intellectual
attainments and a wider field of usefulness for women.

All the different schemes and varied opinions in regard to female education may be reduced to two conflicting
theories, to one or the other of which they all belong.   Whatever may be arguments presented or the claims made, they
belong to one of these two theories.   One is conservative, the
other progressive.   One is heathen, the other Christian.   One
is the old heathen idea that woman is made to be a servant,
that she is to be educated as a servant and that there is but

one sphere of which a woman may occupy with honour, that is the domestic circle. The other, the Christian theory, shows us that the object of existence here is the cultivation and the development of the soul, that women are not merely machines made to play all the same part, but that they are human beings having diversities of gifts, faith, ..., all destined for Heaven or capable of attaining spiritual excellence and it is the business of education to bring out and develop all that is highest and best in the soul.

Let us look for a moment at the first of these theories. It has been well expressed by one, the most celebrated educator of the present time, in an address to the class of young ladies on their graduation day. He told them that their only sphere of usefulness was the domestic circle, that women were to be educated for that, for that alone. They were to be taught facts but not reasons, results, but not process, history but not mathematics. Most of the courses of education in our female seminaries, the popular books and lectures on the sphere and duties of woman ... are based upon this theory. The common conversation in society, the instruction given by wise mothers and successful teachers is a part of the same. In this respect we are heathens. We have not accepted the sublime teachings of Christ. Society, like Martha of old, still asks that woman should be commanded to serve. It frowns upon all efforts to attain for women better opportunities for gaining knowledge or experience and is content to educate all for the duties of the domestic. The result of this is that the course of education pursued is narrow, imperfect and incomplete. It leaves the higher faculties of the soul unmotivated. It dwarfs and belittles the mind. It takes away self-respect, kills out ambition, destroys hope. It leaves the reasoning faculties wholly undeveloped. It says plainly that the beneficient creation has implanted in the mind of woman powers which are unnecessary and superfluous which are not designed for cultivation or use but which it is the business of education to eradicate. It professes to prepare women for the most solemn responsibilities and the most important duties for the guiding and directing of the minds of the future statesmen and philosophers, the development of immortal souls. And yet it denies the need of thorough intellectual training, professes to fill the mind with facts but not to discipline it for meeting the trials and emergences of life, to polish and refine but not to strengthen and develop. Women are taught what is called the accomplishments, all that is necessary to make them entertaining and pleasing but not that which fits them for independent steering of their

course through the difficulties of life. You are to learn just
enough said a teacher of chemistry to his class, enabling you
to appear intelligent. To appear intelligent, to seem beautiful, to displease no one, is the problem presented to every
young woman.

Is it any wonder then that women, who are educated
to be weak and silly and artificial and dependent so frequently
make injudicious ... mothers, wholly unfit for the responsibilities they have assumed and the duties which are laid upon
them?

But if the popular course of female education were
eminently successful in the work it professes to do, if it ef-
ficiently prepared many women to fulfill their duties in the
domestic life, its results would still be injurious since in a
community like ours it educates thousands of people for positions which they will never occupy. ... Women are sent into
the world to do their part in its work, to share in its trials
and to bear its burdens without real knowledge or experience,
without the power of reasoning, without courage and in every
way unprepared for the positions which they are to fill. They
have been taught that they are to be protected but they have
no protector. They have been instructed in the means of
rendering themselves pleasing and their homes agreeable but
they have no homes to make pleasant, no one upon whom to
depend and the art of being agreeable is not sufficient of itself to provide for their wants and supply them with food and
clothing, to furnish means of culture and improvement and
to render them independent and happy. The conflicts of this
world of business call for sterner qualities than mere good
nature and politeness. Those women want the vigor, the
energy, the ambition and the courage of their brothers and
lacking this, their lives become too often a miserable failure.
We find earnest ones struggle along gaining a miserable pittance by some kind of work or employment which is considered suitable for women. A great many are content to remain as humble dependents upon some benevolent families in
which they occupy a position little better than the servant,
little lower than the children. Some are reduced to want,
to beggary, to shame and to sin. This is no imaginary or
fanciful reality. The statistics of crime in our larger cities
show full and plainly that the great majority of erring women
are those who have been unfitted by their kind of education
to depend upon themselves and being left without means of
support have turned to the only resort that was open to them.
The old mode of educating young women merely to become

agreeable and useful in the domestic [rather than to] fit them
for life with its duties and responsibilities, makes them of
necessity feeble, dependent creatures of circumstance, the
victim of the condition in which they are placed.   Every
woman who is dependent upon herself for support and happiness knows the truth of what I say.   Every soldier's widow,
suddenly deprived of her support and dependency and thrown
upon her own resources will confirm it.   It is not enough to
learn to be agreeable in your home.   She [who] struggles in
the rude jostles of the world [requires] mental discipline,
energy, perseverance, self-denial, knowledge of life and
power to see the course of things.   The responsibilities of
the teacher and the mother require all these.   And whatever
her position [she] has need of all the knowledge, all the experience and all the discipline which she can command.   It
is not enough to learn facts and results.   Where is the woman
to be found that does not need to trace the causes of what she
sees and to understand processes.   If we consider only this
world and ask utility alone, we shall be unsatisfied with the
old theory of education.   It does not answer the demands of
the age.   It fails to meet the experiences and needs of women
but there is still a graver objection.   It recognizes no <u>soul</u>
in woman.   It leaves out of account the future, higher life.
It does not seek, does not propose to attain the highest possible development of which woman is capable, does not ask
whether such a course of study or life conduces to spiritual
growth or whether it makes a noble character or a Christ-
like human being, but only whether it fits one to be a good
wife.   It recognizes women only as servants and seeks only
to perfect them as such.   Those who advocate and uphold this
system are in the same condition with the learned men of
Russia.   Some years ago when they met to gravely consider
the subject whether it could be probable that women have
souls, they seem to class them with the lower animals who
knew no improvement, no spiritual growth, who are all alike
and who complete their mission in this life instead of regarding them as human beings with God-given souls destined for
immortality.   But we turn from the wrong and injustice produced by a false theory of education and an evil prejudice in
society to the words and teachings of Christ.   He brings life
and hope to all.   He speaks to women of the joys of eternal
life, of reconciliation with the father, of the beauties of holiness and of the promises of the future.   It was to a woman
that he first revealed himself as the Messiah, declaring the
glad tidings of great joy, teaching that worship was no longer
to be confined to a few at Jerusalem but that like at Samaria
and at Jerusalem the father seeketh those who may worship

him in spirit and in truth. It was to Mary that he unfolded
not facts alone but the great principles which underlie society,
the mysteries of God's providence, the wonders of his love.
And as she listened to his words, delighting in the truths he
taught, she chose knowledge, Christian truth for her portion
and from that time the word went forth that Christianity
brought freedom to woman, freedom to think, to speak, to
learn, the truths of nature and the revelations which God
makes to his children, freedom to develop and cultivate all
the powers of the soul, freedom to seek, to struggle and improve every power or good. He broke the chains of their
servitude and bade them choose liberty and light. He taught
them to live not for time, but for eternity, not merely to
please the world and to be agreeable but to do the will of
the Lord. Not to think upon what they should eat and what
they should drink or wherein they should be clothed, but to
seek first the kingdom of God and his righteousness. It was
a sinful woman who washed his feet with her tears and wiped
them with the hairs of her head and he said her sins were
forgiven for she loved so much. He pronounced no condemnation upon any particular class but he offers hope to all.

Christianity condemns wrongdoing regardless of the
condition, the position or the character of the sinner. Christ
knows no distinction of persons. He revealed himself alike
to men and women. He taught them the same principles to
guide them in their daily lives and to point them on to heaven.
He spoke as never a man spoke, exhorting men and women
alike to labour not for meat that perisheth but for that meat
which endureth unto everlasting life. A Christian education
then must be one which aims to develop all the highest powers
of the soul, which fits one not only for the duties of the world
but for the joys of heaven. The mechanic or housekeeper is
not merely a labourer but a living soul, a thinking, reasoning being holding communion with God and allied to the angels. No one should be content with a mere preparation for
his worldly business. But everyone should nourish the mind
with knowledge and wisdom and cultivate the soul by medita-
tion upon the wonderful works of God. A Christian educator
will not ask whether the student is man or woman, high or
low, but what are the tastes, capacities and needs of the individual. And a Christian civilization will close no avenue
to usefulness, no door to culture and improvement against
women. On the contrary, that can only be a true state of
society which offers to all opportunities for mental discipline
and moral culture which brings religious instruction and education to the schools and the various employments within the

reach of all. It is not enough that the common schools should be free to all. It is not sufficient merely that women should be invited to our colleges. There is a broader and truer education which we get in the world of business, in the various professions and the countless employments which occupy the attention of middle age. It is an unjust and a cruel, wicked thing to [not] educate a human being for a broad sphere of usefulness, to awaken the love of knowledge, to arouse a noble ambition and then to close every avenue ... or chance for the exercise of their talent or their genius.... I remember one young lady who was faithfully pursuing a long course of study in the hope of being thoroughly prepared for any position which she might choose to fill. Energetic, earnest, ambitious, she left school full of hope and determination. She wrote me afterwards from one of our large cities almost in despair. She said, "I can find nothing to do. I have traveled the length and breadth of the city, from early morning till late at night, day after day in search of employment but found none." In such a working world as this, in a country where there is so much to be done in every direction, there is something radically wrong when there is no place for educated women. Christianity applied to our civilization would break down these barriers. Do away with false and unjust prejudice and leave every one free to follow the inspiration of her own genius and the dictates of conscience. As it is it remains for women to improve every means for improvement, to see the most complete education and to embrace every opportunity for widening their sphere of usefulness and expanding new fields of elevating and remunerative employment. We must help one another here. It is sometimes said that woman finds her greatest enemy in those of her own sex. I do not believe it. I believe that the heart of the true woman sympathizes with every movement which is [assisting] the elevation of woman. And many the one in the retirement of her home is silently praying for the success of our cause. A few days ago I saw in one of our religious papers an article exhorting women to save their earnings and contribute it toward educating young men for the ministry, but my friends, charity begins at home. There are young women all over this country whose souls are thirsting for knowledge, who desire a more complete education than their means will allow, who love science and literature and philosophy and whom a little aid and encouragement would enable to take their places among the most brilliant lights in the world of letters. It is these that need the aid of Christian women. The prejudices of society are against them. They are hedged around by false customs, false ideas of woman's duties and education. They are shut out from the means of helping themselves. Their small pay and the narrow sphere in which they move prevents them from rising. And it is to Christian women that they must look for aid, encouragement and cooperation. Let us not despair because we see great evils about us, for the truth is advancing and we look forward to a brighter day. Already there are earnest words spoken for justice. There are true souls pleading for the right across the water. The calm, clear reasonings of John Stuart Mill are convincing the minds of candid, thinking men in power. In our own land there are generous, noble men east and west who are helping forward this cause. The teachings of the New Testament are finding their way to the hearts of all. The words of Christ are beginning to be applied to the subject of woman's education and duties and every year in the future will see a step taken in advance. Then my sisters choose the good part. Choose an enlightened mind, an educated conscience, a noble soul and rest assured that it shall never be taken away.

Services at the Ordination and Installation of
Rev. Phebe A. Hanaford

It becomes my privilege, as the representative of the order
to which we belong, to extend to you the fellowship of the
churches and of the ministers representing our denomination.

You have entered upon a work most important in its
results--a work most glorious when contemplated in regard
to its final results upon the human race--a work of labor,
and often one of trial. You will be called to scenes of sorrow and mourning; it will be yours to weep with those who
weep, as well as to rejoice with those who rejoice, to sympathize with suffering in its various forms. And it will be
your privilege to do this, and all the duties which fall to you,
in reliance upon Him in whom is all your trust. It will be
yours to instruct the young. It will be yours, sometimes,
to offer words of rebuke; to administer words of warning;
for the Gospel comes as a warning against all sin. It knows
no respect of persons; when you preach it, you are to preach
it fearlessly. Someone has said, "Hew to the line, let the
chips fall where they may"; and this seems to me a fitting
precept to be applied to this work. Have no fear, then, in
presenting these truths which Jesus taught, but apply them
wherever there may be occasion and necessity. Jesus knew
no distinction of persons. He used but one code of morals;
sin was sin, wherever found, and it is for you to call as to
the same standard of excellence which Jesus Christ himself
presented. Sin is not to be overlooked because excused by
society in a certain class; but men and women, whoever and
wherever they be, alike need to be called to purity and holiness of life. Spare no position or sex, but reprove, rebuke,
exhort with all long-suffering and doctrine.

As a woman, you stand in some sense as a representative; as one the earliest to assume the high office of the
preacher, it is yours to maintain the position in which you

67

now stand. Remember the words you heard from the Scripture, "Let no man despise you." In your office, show yourself worthy of your high calling. Perfect yourself in the performance of those duties assigned to you. Be faithful, devoted and earnest. Assume every duty, every prerogative
which pertains to the minister, and let it be your purpose
to discharge them as well. Let no one have occasion to say
that you have come short in one particular, even the small-
est of the duties which pertain to the Christian ministry.

It will be yours, as a woman, to sympathize with and
aid suffering women, who needs the sympathies of her sex.

It will be yours to strengthen those who suffer from
the evil influences of the use of intoxicating drinks. Give
them the hand of helping, and lift them up out of their sad
estate.

Young women will look to you for instruction and guid-
ance--for that sympathy which they have not found in the ministry in the years that are past. Be it yours to call them
to a higher life. Jesus died for women--for all--to make
known to us the Gospel; to make us free in that liberty which
the Gospel alone can give. It will be yours to call these
young women to the earnest defence of the Word, to awaken
in them a true life, to teach them to live for God and humanity. And my prayer is, that you will have opportunity
to lead some of the young women of your parish to consecrate themselves to the work of the ministry. I would that
you might lead them up, to be sharers with us in this work.

In your work you are not unaided or alone. You are
upheld by the most glorious faith that was ever revealed to
the children of men; it will be to you inspiration and help.
It will enable you to speak with authority because you speak
of the same glad tidings that were published by Jesus Christ
eighteen hundred years ago. You have always the consciousness of the presence of Jesus, and you may feel, too, that
the great cloud of unseen witnesses, spirits of the departed,
of the fathers of our faith and of lovers of truth in all ages
are hovering near, speaking to your soul.

And more visible, but not more real, stand the great
company of living witnesses, the whole household of your
faith, dear brothers and sisters, who are praying for our
success, earnest preachers of the Gospel who have preceded
you in the Lord's work; grave D. D. s who hail with joy the

coming of another devoted laborer; professors in our theological schools who should see in each cultured preacher of the word an added power for education and for faith.   Young students of divinity who will look up to you as an example and a leader; all these will be with you in this glorious cause and in the name of all these, as their representatives, I today offer you the right hand of fellowship of the Universalist denomination.   You shall have our cooperation,   our sympathy,   our best wishes and our prayers.

You are welcome to the work--welcome to the labors, welcome to the triumphs, welcome to the sacrifices (for there are sometimes, yes, oftentimes, sacrifices to be made by the Christian minister), welcome to the rewards and the joys that come from the consciousness of doing good.   And may it be that your ministry with us, will be long and richly blest. May God prosper you; may you see the fruits of your work, blossoming here about you like the sweet spring flowers, carrying joy to your heart, and to the heart of the beholder. Amen.

Read Before the Ministerial Union
Published by Request

Has woman any place in the church? If so, how is the place
to be determined, and what should be her position in relation
to the cause of truth and religion? The ancient Jews said
woman has no place in the church; they did not recognize her
as a moral and spiritual being, accountable to God and under
obligations to work for the truth; there was for her no part
in the public worship, and no place in the synagogue. In an
outer court, separated from the rest by a rail, women might
stand, and, peeping through, catch a glimpse of those services by which their brothers were to be edified and instructed.
The different ancient nations, so far as we know, failed to
recognize the need of spiritual culture in woman. They
sometimes admitted women to a place in their religious pro-
cessions, or, like the Greeks, at times made her the invol-
untary instrument through which some oracular sayings were
given to the world; but even then she was but an instrument
in the hands of cunning priests. It was not as a responsible
worker for the good of society, nor for her own spiritual
good, that she was admitted to any part in the ceremonies
of religion.

It was for Christ, first in the history of the world,
to recognize woman as worthy of the respect, the liberty,
and the obligations that belong to a human being. He saw
her capability of grasping those great principles which lie
at the basis of the absolute religion, and of applying those
principles to the needs of the world.

Nothing else so distinguished the Christian religion
from all other systems as its recognition of the feminine element. Other systems took note of strong, able, and free
men; Christianity cared for the humble, the poor, and the
oppressed. It broke the shackles which the old barbarous
law of might makes right had imposed upon woman. It rec-

70

ognized the feminine element in human society and made it a power for good.

It has been said that the character of Jesus was essentially a feminine character. It foreshadowed a new type of manhood, in which the test of excellence should be no longer physical strength, but moral power and spiritual discernment.

Accordingly, we find the prophecies of the Old Testament speaking of a condition of society in which the prevailing spirit shall be gentleness and charity and peace, when the "lion and the lamb shall lie down together, and a little child shall lead them."

The Old Testament Scriptures constantly look forward to a new era for woman. Early we find the prediction that the seed of the woman shall bruise the serpent's head, indicating that while, through disobedience, sin and misery were entailed upon the race, through woman was to come the redemption. Christianity was to find in the emancipation of woman its grandest triumph over the great enemy of the race. In the old dispensation, woman was to suffer, to toil, to be ruled over, and to submit in sorrow; in the new dispensation she was to stand as a victorious queen, having put all enemies under her feet, and gained the salvation of the world.

Christ, possessing all feminine characteristics, ushering in the reign of gentleness and peace, was at once the representative of man and woman. Like the great, infinite Being, whose vicegerent he was, he combined all the excellences of male and female character in himself, and his system made no distinction of sex in respect to sphere of labor or moral obligations. The prophet Joel, looking forward to the great changes which would be effected through Christianity, said, "I will pour out my spirit upon all flesh, and your sons and your daughters shall prophesy." And I recall, too, that grand prophecy contained in the last chapter of Proverbs, a description, I believe, yet to be realized, when the Christian woman, free, enlightened, endowed with all rights of the citizen, shall take her place in the Master's vineyard, girded with strength and honor, her mouth filled with words of wisdom and her own works praising her in the gates.

When Christ came, in accordance with the words of prophecy, he opened a new world to woman. Truly, in the new dispensation, God did pour out his spirit upon woman.

Christ first revealed himself as the promised Messiah
to a woman; it was at a woman's request that he performed
the first miracle; he admitted women to listen to his instruc-
tions, and to cooperate with him in carrying the glad tidings
of salvation to a sorrowing world. It was Mary who sat at
Jesus' feet and conversed with him of the lofty themes which
engaged his attention. It was women who were last at the
cross and first at the sepulchre. It was a woman who was
first commissioned to preach the risen Saviour, --"Go, tell
my disciples that I am risen from the dead"; and if Jesus
did not choose women among the twelve who were to be his
immediate followers, it was rather owing to the peculiarities
of the times, than to any unfitness in woman herself. We do
not seek in our ministers and church-members a likeness to
the disciples in merely personal matters; we do not ask that
they shall be all Jews, all fishermen, or tax-gatherers; that
they shall correspond in color of hair or eyes with the teacher, --it was not these little particulars, nor yet the fact that
they were men, which fitted the original twelve to be Christ's
disciples; but it was that they were earnest and loyal to the
truth, and filled with the Holy Spirit; and wherever there is
man or woman, bond or free, Jew or Gentile, who has received this spirit, there is one whom Christ has chosen, and
who is worthy to go forth to labor in his cause. And immediately after the coming of Christ, we find woman taking
a new position, making a part of all public congregations,
entering into public discussions to such an extent that the
Apostle Paul found it necessary to rebuke those who were
ignorant and not accustomed to so much liberty, and were
taking up the time with foolish questions; but in many places
he commends those who labored in the church, as when he
sent Phebe forth as a minister of the church at Cenchrea,
applying to her the same term which he applies to himself
when he calls himself a minister of the New Testament: and
not only does he command her, but he exhorts the friends at
Rome to cooperate with her in her labors as a minister, --
all showing that even at this early day women were found engaging in the gospel work. In the early Christian Church,
we are told that women shared in the public services equally
with men. Hase says that in the meetings of the early Christians women took part in the same forms of worship with
men; and another historian says that in these meetings of the
early church, "all addressed the audience as they were moved,
not excepting women"; and in the part of the work which we
call pastoral labor, women were found to be efficient. The
office of deaconess was early established, by which women
were formally set apart for the Christian work, consecrated

by the imposition of hands, a ceremony in all respects similar to the ordination ceremony of the present day; and their
duties consisted in visiting and praying with the sick, in con-
versing with the new converts, --in fact, all that we mean by
the pastoral labor of the preacher came within their jurisdiction: and from that time to this, in different departments of
the Christian Church, women have been worthy workers.

Those churches which have accomplished most have
been those which have most availed themselves of woman's
earnest religious spirit and ready cooperation in the cause
of truth.

The Catholics have been too wise to cut themselves
off from such a source of power; but by their deification of
the Virgin, by the appointment of women to offices in the
church, offering a sphere of activity to those who wished to
consecrate themselves to the cause of religion, they have
gained for themselves a wonderful power. Take away all
this, all the tenderness and sacredness which attaches to
their idea of the Virgin, all the good, benevolent works of
the Sisters of Charity, all the opportunities of culture which
are afforded in their convents, all the power they have gained
by their use of woman's ability, and it is safe to conclude
that at least two-thirds of the influence of the Catholic Church
would be gone.

The Methodists, the most rapidly increasing of any
Protestant denomination, owe much of their power to the
prominence which they have given to women, permitting them
to speak, to exhort, or to pray in their public meetings; ap-
pointing them as class-leaders; and in various ways making
them an instrumentality of promulgating their faith.

The Quakers, though not a growing denomination, owing to their peculiarities of dress and manner, have never-
theless exerted a great influence in favor of reform; and their
most efficient workers, their most able preachers, have always been women, --their most inspired utterances have fallen
from women's lips. And among philanthropists and preachers
the world has seen few nobler examples than Lucretia Mott
and Elizabeth Fry. Indeed, since Christ came and declared
himself first of all to a woman, sending women forth to proclaim his resurrection, women have found a place in the
Christian Church.

Society needs woman's influence, the church needs her.

If, as some claim, she has more of intuition, more of spiritual vision than man, the church needs that; if she is more
apt to teach, more sympathetic and gentle, the church needs
those qualities; and we want all these different gifts, the
firmness, the decision, the power of argument, the force
of logic, the "pure thought" which is said to characterize
man, and also the spirituality, the moral force, the tact,
the keenness of perception, which are usually attributed to
woman. If man and woman are counterparts of each other,
unlike in mental capacity, and differing in their experiences,
then we cannot get our greatest power or do our full work
until man and woman cooperate, each supplying those qualities which are deficient in the other.

God has placed man and woman together in the world
in families and in society; they modify each other, and the
great facts of human experience, the great needs of the world,
cannot be comprehended until man's observation and reason
are supplemented and made complete by woman's perception
and ready inference. It has been said, I know, that there is
too much sentiment about religion already, and that woman
would make it more so. But it may be that man in our divinity schools and ministerial meetings, shut out from the influence of woman's mind, endeavoring to grasp a subject for
which he alone is insufficient has fallen into a dawdling sen-
timentality, which, as it is morbid and affected, is wanting
in vigor and in power for good.

I remember a young theologian once, in answer to the
argument that woman's peculiar traits of mind were needed
in the ministry, replied that when God called a man to the
ministry, he created a man with a feminine soul, --and that
expresses the difficulty with the ministry today: it is too
much composed of men who are trying to put on feminine gentleness and spirituality. We want no monstrosities in the
ministry, no men with feminine souls: let us have the strongest, bravest, best thought of which the masculine mind is capable, and, too, the loftiest inspiration, and the clearest vision, which has been given to woman; and then, if we have
sentiment, it will be genuine, healthful, life-giving.

The fact that at least two-thirds of all our church-
members are women, that in many Sunday schools nearly all
the teachers are women, that in many cases the finances of
the society are largely managed by women, shows full plainly
that woman is adapted to the Christian work.

Thus the voice of prophecy, the example of Christ, the teaching and conduct of the apostles and early Christians, the nature of woman's mind, and the needs of the church and the world, all combine to prove that woman has rightfully, by every law of God, a place in the church. There may be a difference of opinion as to what that place should be. Some ask that woman should be allowed to work in the church, wherever her taste or capacity may lead; that she may preach or pray, or labor, as God shall call her: but others, while admitting that woman is eminently adapted to Christian work, would still deny her all opportunity to preach that gospel which has emancipated her from slavery. There are those who see in her a valuable instrumentality in promoting the prosperity and increasing the power of the church, who avail themselves of her peculiar gifts to swell their numbers and establish their institutions, who yet close the pulpit as a place too sacred for such unhallowed associations. There are those who seem to think that woman's place in the church is to carry on the Sunday school, to conduct the sewing society, to raise money for missionary enterprises, to add life to the prayer and conference meetings, to get good dinners for the ministers, in fact, to do anything and everything pertaining to ministerial work, except to receive the recognition and take the salary. Our Methodist brethren were recently discussing whether they could recognize as a minister a certain Mrs. Van Coot, who by her preaching had made two thousand converts to their faith. I did not learn whether they proposed to reject the two thousand converts made by such unholy means. And in my own denomination, while much has been said against women in the ministry, I have never heard that anyone has objected to using the thousands of dollars collected by Mrs. Livermore, as she has gone here and there, holding meetings and speaking of our blessed faith. In the midst of such conflicting opinions in regard to woman's true place in the church, it might be well to ask what tribunal shall decide, and how shall we ascertain her sphere of labor? I would suggest that it cannot be determined by any class of persons differently constituted from woman, nor by any class having different experiences from her own. Man, from the nature of the case, is incompetent to decide for woman, since his different mental characteristics unfit him for comprehending her capacities or knowing what are her inclinations.

It cannot be determined entirely by past experience, because every age develops new needs in society and new methods of working; besides, the more liberal education and larger opportunities which the present time offers to woman enable her to prepare herself for usefulness in a manner unknown in the past.

It being granted that the subject of religion is one of interest to woman, and that, in accordance with right and revelation, she has some place in the Christian Church, it remains only to give her freedom of choice as to what that place shall be.

Encourage her to labor in the cause of truth; give her every opportunity of preparation, and, placing her on precisely the same footing with men, leave her free to work in the pulpit or out of it, and then let God decide where her true place shall be; for when perfect freedom and fair opportunity are given, she will follow out the law of her nature, and that nature will not long suffer itself to be outraged by a disobedience to its promptings.

It is my own opinion, as a woman of seven years' experience in the ministry, that the work of the minister is peculiarly suited to woman, and that the great need of the present time is women in the clerical profession. Just what we want to give life to our churches, and awaken the people to effort, is the enthusiasm and the heart which earnest, devoted, educated women could bring to the work. This is shown by the success which attends the preaching of women of very moderate ability and most meagre preparation; it is shown by the fact that Mrs. Van Coot, without any special preparation, in the short space of a few months, can bring two thousand persons into the Methodist Church. It is shown by the wonderful effect which is produced among the Spiritualists, by women without education or peculiar fitness, who, freed from all restraint by the pleasing delusion that they are influenced by spirits, simply speak what they feel. Let those women feel that they are just as free to speak for themselves as they are for the spirits, that they are inspired only by the great spirit of truth; let them be educated and prepared to instruct the people, --and their power for good would become almost incalculable. The time has come when God calls woman into this vineyard; the fields are all white and ready for the harvest.

If there are some portions of the pastoral labor which man can perform better than woman, there are also some which woman can perform better than man.

There are weak, sinful, sorrowing women to be re-
formed and comforted; and it is not a thing unheard of that
the minister, in performance of the delicate task imposed
upon him, has been betrayed into courses of action which he
has had reason to regret: the character described by Holmes
in his "Guardian Angel" is not unknown in the ministry, and
every such case is a new argument in favor of women in the
capacity of pastors of societies.   Indeed, where is the organization of men from which women are excluded which has
long remained pure? Every profession needs the cooperation
of men and women.   But it is contended that the profession
conflicts with woman's other duties, and that her domestic
life is incompatible with the work of the minister.

This is the same argument upon which the Church in
past times required the celibacy of the clergy, although it is
brought with a greater show of reason in the case of woman.

But, even if admitted, it cannot apply to all women:
the number of men who enter the ministry is small, when
compared with the whole, and there are women enough who
are not engaged in domestic duties to supply all the pulpits
in the land. Besides, if, here and there, a woman is found
who is occupying at once the position of a mother of a family
and a minister of the gospel, such cases will settle themselves as they arise, and the compatibility will depend upon
the versatility of the individual and the nature of the duties
imposed.

We have no reason to fear that women will engage in
a profession prejudicial to the interests of those that God has
committed to their keeping.   The good Father has not so
lightly drawn the chords of affection in the mother's heart.
It is a libel upon God and nature to suppose that a woman
would forsake a loved husband or children for any position
which the world can give.   Nor need we fear that time spent
in the preparation for the ministry will be lost, even should
other cares come in to engross the attention; for the mother
needs the widest range of culture and the most complete mental discipline.   Nothing is ever learned in vain.   Antoinette
Brown presides in her home all the more gracefully, and educates her four little girls all the more judiciously, that her
mind has been trained, and her knowledge of human nature
increased, by years of study and labor in the clerical profession.   Lucretia Mott appeals to our hearts all the more
potently, that, as the mother of a large family, she has had
an experience which has called out her deepest and holiest

feelings, and taught her the mysterious wealth of our God-
given human nature.

The hour draws nigh when the gospel shall find its
most efficient preachers, Christianity its most devoted laborers, among women.

The time is ripe for work. The great West, with its
millions of enterprising, progressive people, is asking for a
liberal Christian faith.

Thousands of unemployed women, wearing out their
lives in unsatisfied yearnings for some noble aim, indicate
the source from which we are to obtain laborers in the cause
of Christ.

Woman, long time waiting amid oppression and ignorance, is, ere long, to arise from her darkness, and, girded
with strength and honor, to go forth to speak words of wisdom for the regeneration of the people, and her own works
shall praise her in the gates. And when we shall see women
calling the people by thousands to lives of purity and holiness,
when through their instrumentality churches shall be established, and the glad tidings of salvation carried to sorrowing
hearts, then will the prophecy be verified, "The seed of the
woman shall bruise the serpent's head. In her shall all the
nations of the earth be blest."

A Sermon Preached at the First Universalist
Church, Bridgeport, Conn.
Printed in Gospel Banner, March 30, 1872

Beloved, if God so loved us, we ought
also to love one another. God is love.

Universalists believe in a God of love. They believe in a
God who looks with the equal eye upon all his children; who
can never be alienated or estranged from any; who ever seeks
the means for the salvation of the world from sin, and who
will ultimately bring every wandering soul home, reconciled
and confirmed in the good.

The Fatherhood of God, the Brotherhood of man--this
is the doctrine by which we are known in the world, from
which our name is derived--the doctrine which first caused
the separation of the fathers of our faith from the partialist
churches; in behalf of which they endured persecution and
condemnation untold--and it was this faith in the Universal
love of God which made them strong to endure and mighty to
prevail against enemies in high places and in low, against
persecution and bigotry and the united force of all the popular, well-organized and wealthy churches of the land. It has
made weak men strong; those who were feeble and halting in
speech grew eloquent under the inspiration of the doctrine of
God's universal love; those who were ignorant and untaught
manifested a power greater than all the learning of the
schools could give, for their minds were illumed by a light
from heaven. The timid and fearful grew confident and bold
when they came to speak of the power of God, to move the
hearts of men and to give them strength at last to triumph
over death and sin. It is this doctrine of God's love for all
his children which is the life of our denomination today--
which distinguished us from all other sects, and which gives
us a wondrous power for good. By it the mourner is com-

forted, the proud heart of the sinner touched, youth stimulated to noble endeavor and old age cheered with the brighter
prospects beyond.   This then is the source of our strength;
it is preeminently our doctrine, identified with all our history, plainly expressed in our confession of faith; it glows
on every page of our denominational works.   It shines out in
every sermon, which has either beauty or excellence.   It is
a constant source of satisfaction and delight to the believer;
the doctrine so plainly taught by prophet and apostle, by the
writers of the Old Testament and the New, embodied in the
whole life of Christ, reiterated again and again by Paul that
"God so loved the world that he gave his only begotten son,
that the world through him might be saved"; that "the Father
sent the son to be a propitiation for our sins and not for ours
only, but for the sins of the whole world."

My text plainly sets forth the duty which such a doctrine imposes.   "Beloved, if God so loved us we ought also
to love one another."   Or, as the prophet Malachi more dra-
matically expresses it, "Have we not all one Father?   Hath
not one God created us?   Why then do we deal treacherously
every man against his brother?"   The new commandment that
"we love one another" was based upon the idea of the universal brotherhood.   It was a consequence deduced logically
and directly from the statement of God's love for all his
children.   If God so loved us we ought also to love one another.   Never could doctrine and duty be more closely allied,
or expressed more distinctly and connectedly than in the
words of the text.   If, indeed, all are one family, if it be
true as the apostle said that "God created of one blood all
the nations of men to dwell in all the face of the earth":   if
we have all one Father, and one God hath created us, and if
he has designed all to dwell with him through the endless
cycles of eternity, how near we are to one another!   How
precious does every soul become!   We feel that every one
is worthy of our love: we dare not [reject] the meanest man
alive.   All are our kindred.   Yonder depraved being, reared
in the haunts of vice, to whom vulgarity and lewdness have
been made familiar by long acquaintance, and the self-
complacent sycophant filled with hypocritical cant, mouthing
pious words, shedding crocodile tears, "going about to establish her own righteousness"; they are both our sisters.
The barbarous heathen in the far off land who knows not the
first principles of Christianity and the successful and responsible heathen in our own land who worships mammon and the
things of this world, the wandering outcast for whom there
is no rest or home, the haughty bigot who feels himself to

be the special favorite of God: these all belong to the same
family--selfish, sinful, debased as they are, God loves them.
They are all endowed with capabilities of holiness, all precious in the sight of him who died for the just, such poor,
deluded beings and the admonition of the Master, ... "that
you despise not one of these little ones" reminds us that he
is watching over them even now, and he bids us love them
all.

We dare not call any man "common or unclean" for
our God is no respector of persons. He has created all in
his image; he surrounds them all with his love and has declared that he will save them all and bring them to the knowledge of the truth. This thought makes men charitable and
just to their fellow beings. When you are tempted to pronounce harsh judgment upon your companions, or to deal un-
justly with any man or to condemn without a hearing, the
thought that the same God has created all and that that condemned, defrauded brother will stand side by side with you
in the heavenly mansion will check the harsh judgment and
stay the unworthy deed. All are God's children, therefore
all should be held sacred. All have a claim upon our sympathy and regard. But if our theory is not the true one and
the men and women around us are not precious in the sight
of God, if they are the children of the devil, their thoughts
and capabilities only evil, their nature wholly depraved and
themselves destined to everlasting condemnation, then they
have no claim upon our charity and the command "love one
another" is shorn of its authority and of its significance. It
becomes a meaningless phrase, a mere glittering generality.
Why should we love the children of Satan? What fellowship
hath righteousness with unrighteousness....

It is because they are not wholly the children of Belial,
not altogether unrighteous that we are to love them....

If they are totally depraved and are not to be our companions in the heavenly mansions but are to be forever condemned, why should we cherish them here? Or what is there
in them to command our respect or awaken our love? In
that case there would be no duty resting upon men to love
[them]....

The duty of charity grows directly out of the fact of
the universal brotherhood of the race. It is only possible in
the light of that truth. There are those so overcome by the
temptation of the world, so enveloped in selfishness that their

characters seem unlovely and charity is only possible when
we contemplate them as the children of the All Father, and
remember that his love never fails, and that he will ultimately redeem from sin and develop them into the symmetry
of the angels.   As God's universal love is the grandest truth
ever revealed to men, the central thought of the whole Christian system, so the corresponding duty to love our fellow
men is the most imperative of any and charity the divinest
of all the virtues.   Hence Paul gave to it such high praise:
"Though I speak with the tongues of men and angels and have
not charity, I am become as sounding brass or a tinkling
cymbal, and though I have the gift of prophecy and understand all mystery and all knowledge and though I have all
faith so that I could remove mountains and have not charity,
I am nothing; and though I bestow all my goods to feed the
poor and though I give my body to be burned and have not
charity it profiteth me nothing."

Peter also pays tribute to the superiority of this virtue, placing it above all the other Christian graces.   In his
letter he says "be sober, watch unto prayer and above all
things have fervent charity among yourselves."   Thus higher
than temperance, devotion, watchfulness and prayer, is charity, and John carries out the same thought for he says "love
is the fulfilling of the law."   He that dwelleth in love dwelleth
in God."   "If we love one another God dwelleth in us," and
Christ lived out the same idea, for we find him always loving, always tolerant, forgiving men's sin and ignorance, associating freely with even the most sinful and condemned while
he taught men that they should not judge one another, and to
the guilty he only said "go and sin no more."   And the sinful woman was forgiven for she loved much.   That one excellence, that one generous sentiment outweighed a whole life
of sin.

Such is the supremacy of love, such the superior place
which the gospel assigns to charity, the highest, the most
Godlike attribute of humanity; the crowning glory of the Christian.

But I find a great want of true conception of charity,
and it may be properly asked what is meant by charity and
how is it manifested?   Charity in the New Testament is synonymous with love.   It means Christian love; that respect and
good will which we are bound to feel for all God's children,
simply on the grounds of their humanity.   It does not necessarily imply almsgiving, nor is it identical with that love

which we feel for our kindred or our countrymen. The
mother loves her children with a great and wondrous tenderness. She is willing to labor, to suffer and even to die
for them; but all this is not charity. The love of father and
mother, sister of brother: the love which we feel for those
of kindred tastes or who are endeared to us by kindly offices
of friendship, is not charity, nor is the gratitude which we
render to those who have benefited us or the admiration with
which we regard those of preeminent virtue; none of those
require to be enforced by command after command based
upon argument and set forth with such high praise,--those
are sentiments which characterize the most selfish and worldly: they mark no high Christian attainment. Anybody could
love the good. It is the office of charity to be kind to the
sinful. The ... savage loves his tribe, his kindred, his
companions. Christian charity reaches for other than this.
The most selfish are grateful for favors received, but Christian love can bless them that curse and do good to them that
hate and pray for them that despitefully abuse and persecute.

"If ye love them which love you," said Christ, "what
reward have ye, do not even the publicans [do] the same?"
Rather be perfect in the love by which your Father in Heaven
"makes His sun to shine upon the evil and upon the good and
sendeth His rain upon the just and the unjust."

Yes, charity means more than that benevolence which
gives alms or that sympathy which pities the weak, or that
reverence which we pay to virtue, or the regard we feel for
friends and kindred. It is that love which the Christian feels
for every human being, because he is a human being, without
any regard to his position, nationality, race, intellectual attainments or moral worth. It is the view he takes of his
fellow men when he occasions to regard them in their relations to himself, when he goes out of himself and views them
as children of the Infinite, fitted with grandest capabilities,
destined to a glorious immortality.

It is the recognition of something worthy of our love
in every bruised and battered, tempest-tossed, sin-stricken
child of God. It is the spiritual eye which looks beyond the
pollution of sin, beneath the hard exterior and sees there the
elements of moral beauty--and in that defaced, blurred soul,
beholds forever the image of his Maker. It binds together
the whole human family, however diverse in characters and
tastes, separated by space or time. It links the ages together by a bond of sympathy, spans the globe with a chain

of love which extends from heart to heart, reaches upward
to the angels and centers at last in God.

Charity is manifested in outward acts, when men provide largely and generously for the comfort or improvement
of their fellow beings.   It recognizes strangers, is hospitable,
and often entertains angels unawares.   Two men wandering
far from home meet in a distant land.   They are each ignorant of the other's history, associations, or position, but
charity makes them friends.   They readily render one another aid and kindly sympathy, and never stop to ask about
differences of rank or culture, or nation.   It metes out exact
justice to men in all conditions, to friend and to enemy alike.
It tolerates the peculiarities and individualities of others and
gives large liberty to men to live out their highest conceptions.   It imposes no fetter, places no stumbling blocks in
another's way, it encourages every effort for the right, however humble and seemingly unsuccessful it may be.

The noblest exhibition of charity is seen when it "covers a multitude of sins" when it credits men not with the
wrong they have done, but with the good they have intended
to do, and looking at the bright side of even the darkest life,
finds there occasion for rejoicing.   Nor is this a confound-
ing of the distinction between virtue and vice.   There is a
noble emulation with which we contemplate the virtuous man.
We look upon him with delight and gather inspiration from his
example.   But charity weeps over sin, while it pities, loves
and strives to reclaim the sinner!   The physician glories in
the strong arm and elastic step of the man of vigorous health.
He contemplates with satisfaction the ruddy glow upon his
cheek and the life and animation manifest in every motion,
but he sees in the invalid, weak, pale, ... a frame governed
by the same laws, created with the same wondrous skill, designed for the same powers and beauty, and he hastens to do
what he can to restore him to health.   So the moral physician, while he glories in the truly virtuous and upright man,
still sees in the tempted and fallen, a brother in possession
of the same immortal soul, but needing human sympathy and
aid.   Nor does it become the Christian to condemn without
consideration.   Says an eminent divine: "The man who is
most charitable is not the man who is himself most lax.
Deep knowledge of human nature tells us it is exactly the
reverse.   He who shows the rough and thorny road to heaven
is he who treads the primrose path himself."   Be sure that
it is the severe and pitiless judge and censor of other faults
on whom at a venture you may safely fix the charge "Thou
art the man."

I know not why, but "unrelenting severity proves guilt
rather than innocence." So Christ thought when the over-
zealous Pharisees brought the guilty woman to be stoned to
death and he only said, "Let him that is without sin among
you cast a stone at her." And again when with such terrible
earnestness, he spoke to the self-righteous hypocrite of that
time, "Woe unto you Scribes, Pharisees and hypocrites for
ye shut up the kingdom of heaven against men. Woe, unto
you Scribes and Pharisees for ye pay tithe of mint, anise and
cumin, and have omitted the weightier matters of the law,
judgment, mercy and faith. Ye blind guides which strain at
a gnat and swallow a camel." Woe unto you Scribes and
Pharisees, hypocrites "for ye make clean the outside of the
cup and of the platter, but within are full of extortion and
excess."

It is easy to pronounce severe condemnation upon a
wrongdoer and to declare your horror of such inequity, but
it is the part of charity to consider the circumstances which
surrounded the guilty one, the motives which prompted to the
act, as Burns has it. "The [motives] why they do it." When
some notorious man like James Fisk has come to be known
far and wide for the magnitude of his wrongdoing and has
met with general condemnation, then it is easy to join in the
general outcry, make your voice heard above all others in
indiscriminate denunciation using severer language than others
have dared to use. Especially is this easy if the man is
dead and can neither reply nor retaliate; but such action
speaks more of a desire to proclaim your own righteousness
than of a genuine enthusiasm for purity and virtue. A true
love of virtue would rather rebuke that spirit of speculation
which marks the age and that iniquitous state of society which
made a James Fisk possible. A true and loving charity would
seek out the influences which have produced such a character,
and while admonishing all to avoid such temptations, would
speak pityingly, and yet hopefully of the dead.

When someone, by a peculiarity of position or doctrine, has encountered public odium or been disgraced in the
ages of the world, then it is easy to get a cheap reputation
for sanctity, by taking up the popular strain, and echoing it
again and again, until you have outdone all competitors in
wholesale denunciations! But Christian charity would bid
you pause and ask through what horrible experience has this
soul passed that it should become so warped? Through what
wandering, tangled paths has it come, until at last it lost its
way in the maze, not knowing the true points of the moral
compass, and dismayed, deluded, ran recklessly on without

guide or goal. Charity says go to the lost and wandering one
and take away the thorns from his path and point out the
course that leads to God and Heaven. Especially is this uncharitable, indiscriminate denunciations easy and popular if
the victim of public odium chances to be a woman, for it is
the most terrible result of woman's subordination that in her
errors she receives no charity from the world and has none
for her own sex. Two moral standards established in our
society makes that unpardonable. Sin in woman, which in
man is regarded as a joke of every day's occurrence, and
when the erring woman most needs pity and wise guidance,
she is cut off from all human sympathy. No gentle charity
seeks to cover her sins or to recognize her struggles for the
right. No sister's hand is extended to lead her back to virtue and to self-respect; and yet, the great master taught us
to love these fallen ones. Forgive them? Yes, "seven times
forgive, yea, and seventy times seven, or till thyself art as
an angel pure."

God rebukes the Phariseeism and uncharitable judgment,
so manifest in the women of our time. He sees them hard,
pitiless, shutting out the tempted from all opportunity of reform, for true it is, "No stumbling block before his little
ones can hurt them, like a cold, hard, human heart." Nothing today so stands in the way of the reformation of sinful
women, as the hard, self-righteousness of their own sex.

Women "shut up the kingdom of Heaven" against one
another; they do not perhaps "devour widow's houses," but
they filch from a poor sister her only treasure--her good
name--and for a pretense make long prayers. God rebukes
their self-righteous hypocrisy. All their efforts for liberty
and enfranchisement are vain and fruitless and will be so until through sorrow and tribulations they have learned that
greatest of all lessons, charity for their own sex. Charity
overcomes evil with its manifestations of sympathy, and seeks
to win and to reclaim the sinner by love. My friends, you
have seen what charity is: how it is distinguished from other
forms of human love; how it is the grandest, the most far-
reaching, most disinterested, most God-like of them all. I
have shown a few of the ways in which it manifests itself.
Your own daily experience will suggest means and opportunities for its exercise in a thousand ways. You may illustrate
that charity which hopeth all things, believeth all things, which
suffereth long and is kind, by a corresponding life.

I have shown you that the duty of charity grows directly

out of our profession of faith as Universalists. We, of all
others, have no right to be uncharitable. Upon us it is laid
to show forth this highest attainment of the Christian. Others,
who believe in a partial salvation, who see in their neighbors
the irreclaimable children of the devil, are consistent when
they denounce without qualification and condemn without a
hearing; but for us, such things are contradictory and absurd.

The Universalist should have charity for all, seeing
he worships a God whose love is over all. When I hear men
talking long and loud about their faith in the common brotherhood and in the salvation of every human being, and then see
them so intolerant, so bigoted and severe, I feel like asking
them, where is your faith? When a little while ago, in a
debate in Congress, Mr. Carpenter said he gloried in the
Declaration of Independence, Mr. Sumner replied, "The Senator should give some effect to what he glories in. I hope
he will not take it all out in glory; I hope he will see that a
little of it is transfused into human rights." So I would say
to the Universalist who glories in the faith, don't take it all
out in glory. See that a little of your faith is transfused
into human sympathy, into generous forgiveness, into a large
Christian charity!

My friends, "put on charity," leave sectarian bigotry
and harsh unrighteous judgment to those of a narrower faith.
God has manifested to us a glimpse of his love. He has
shown us how that love is around all his children, and how
it will, at last, overcome all sin and draw all men to himself. Oh, let us rejoice and exult and go forth saying of all
God's works that they are very good, and of man, the last,
the best creation, that he is worthy the divine hand that fashioned him.

How should we overcome petty prejudices of sect or
race or condition, and find a brother in every man--

> Break free your bonds, your minds expand
> Take each Sectarian by the hand,
> A Brother be to brother man,
> Their faults forgiven
> And earth shall be a happy land,
> A path to Heaven.
>
> Hail the bright day that shall give birth
> When peace and love shall dwell on earth

And deep to answer and deep shout forth
That man is free
And reign round each domestic hearth
Faith, Hope and Charity.

But you will not always find it easy to exercise charity.   Had it been of easy attainment, something calling for
no discipline and self-sacrifice, Paul [would] not place it
above faith and knowledge, and self-consecration.   It is not
easy to see in the hard selfish and worldly man that spiritual
nature which shall transform him into an angel of light.   It
is hard to see goodness and beauty through an exterior of
drunkenness and vulgarity.   And above all it is most difficult
to recognize and acknowledge the excellencies of those who
have injured or misrepresented and persecuted you.   All this
is difficult; it almost seems, at times, impossible and it can
only come by prayer and watchfulness and deep communion
with him whose very nature is love.   And when you have, in
part, overcome yourself and are able to look with charity
upon some unfortunate, tempted one, you will perchance be
misunderstood.   Your motives will be assailed by the self-
righteous; the superficial will accuse you of laxity ... of
consorting with sinners.   All these things you must expect.
Your master suffered the same when on earth.   The Pharisees of his time were ever ready to assail and accuse him
that he ate with publicans and sinners.   Are you so much
better and wise than he that you should walk unscathed and
applauded the path betrod with bruised feet amid all the bit-
terness of persecution?   Ah no! You must labor and suffer
with him, if you would reign with him.   There are proud
Pharisees still, and if you are following the Master be sure
you will encounter their opposition and often hear their scorn-
ful revilings, but then you have to remember that there is a
power in love to conquer even this, to touch the heart of the
most intolerant persecutor, to win all at last to holiness.
By charity the followers of the Prince of Peace must conquer.   All true victories are to be achieved by its magic
power.   Love is the talisman by which the spirits of evil
shall be driven out, pride and hate overcome and all souls
reconciled at last. ...

THE HIGHER EDUCATION OF WOMEN
(February 1874)

Published in The Repository (Feb. 1874)

Among the subjects proposed for consideration at the recent
Woman's Congress was "the Higher Education of Women," a
subject which embraces all that we seek for woman.   For education, in its largest sense, means not merely the curricu-
lum of the schools, the jargon of science, or the refinements
of literature, it is something more than the memorizing of
facts and dates, names and terms.   It means rather the exact
training of every faculty, and that full development of all the
powers, which shall fit one for largest usefulness in the world.

Higher education looks to the supremacy of all that is
noblest and best in human nature; it means that quickening of
the moral sense, that opening of the spiritual eye which makes
one not merely an efficient worker in the business of the
world, but one of the immortals, a companion of the angels.
In the higher education of women we seek that which shall
make them noble characters.

At the present day too many women, even of good culture, confound character with reputation; and think it of little
consequence what they really are, if they can only manage to
make a fair show before the world.

Now there is a very broad distinction to be made between character and reputation.   Character is what God thinks
of us; reputation is what men say about us.   A good character
is the result of years of discipline and experience, of watchfulness and self-denial; a good reputation is often gained by
a single lucky chance, or may be attained [by] the intrigues
and management of a charlatan or a hypocrite.   Sometimes
by the misjudgment of the multitude, or a false public opinion,
an act in itself bad will gain for the doer a good reputation;
and the same action which gives a bad reputation at one period
may be chief cause of one's glory at another.

Reputation is ever changing; it is one thing today, another thing tomorrow. Dependent upon the caprice of a fickle multitude, a word, a hint, sometimes even a look is sufficient to destroy it. But character is a treasure beyond the reach of the world; it abides through all time and change; it is ours after this world with its transient excitements shall have passed away; it must be the chief source of our power and peace here, as well as of our hopes for the hereafter.

How important, then, that women should secure for themselves noble characters! It is not desirable to gain for them better reputations. The reputation of women is already better than their characters will warrant. Let us seek rather for women that complete knowledge and that thorough discipline by which they may attain unto the measure of the stature of perfect womanhood. Nor is it sufficient that women shall maintain their character for chastity alone; there are other virtues not less valuable to themselves and far more important in their effect upon their dealings with others.

The common use of the term "bad character," meaning an unchaste woman, leads to the inference that all others are good characters, whereas there are very bad characters who have never violated one of the accepted rules of propriety and who possess unsullied reputations. I have heard a woman with vain and self-righteous boasting, exalting herself as a spotless character. She said she had been called almost everything, she had been called cross, and coarse, and profane, but her character had never been attacked. And this illustrates the idea which many women have of what constitutes character. They think they can violate every principle of honor, prove recreant to every duty, false to every dictate of truth or of Christian morality, and yet while they remain chaste their characters are unsullied. Many women will be guilty of acts of cruelty and injustice, of falsehoods and hypocrisies, which would ruin the standing of an ordinary business man, and yet boast of good characters and unsullied reputations. And this not because women are worse than men, not because they are incapable of the highest moral and spiritual attainments, but because from infancy the standard of morality presented to them has been entirely different from that presented to men. They have been taught to cherish one virtue as preeminent above all others. They have been taught that in maintaining what is called "purity" in society, any sacrifice of truth or of charity is allowable.

I have lately had occasion to observe an instance in

which a woman, upon suspicion of something wrong in the conduct of another woman who was travelling as an agent, made haste to write letters of warning to several different cities, giving such intimations, as if believed would bring disgrace upon the agent, besides ruining her success in business. When called to account for this, she wrote a letter which came under my eye. In this she admitted that she had heard nothing and knew nothing against the agent, but had acted wholly on suspicions based on trifles; and yet she had done all in her power to injure the woman. In her letter there was no humility; she wholly ignored her own want of charity in drawing an evil inference from trifling circumstances, and her guilt in slandering and recklessly injuring the reputation and business of another woman, and with lofty condescension assured the woman that if she should prove herself innocent, the suspicions could do her no harm. This woman claims to be a Christian, a leader of reform, and yet apparently fails to see the injustice, cruelty, and downright wickedness of her course.

Among men such unjust inferences, and wicked slander, would bring discredit and severe condemnation; among women it passes current, and even adds to their saintliness because it is all done in the interest of purity. Any degree of falsehood, any misrepresentation of facts, any denunciation of the innocent, any underhand intriguing for the injury of others, is regarded as trifling when compared with the one sin for which society holds a woman guilty. Indeed it would almost seem that all other sins might be committed with honor if done by way of showing a holy zeal for "purity." But what narrowness and meanness is begotten by this one-sided view of duty and of character! It kills out conscience and makes a woman so little regardful of the rights of others and of her obligations to society, as to be willing to live in idleness while father or husband is taxed to the utmost, working from early morning till late at night to keep her in exquisite attire. All unconscious of the true meaning of a noble womanhood, she devotes her life to fashionable follies, to gew-gaws, and petty deceits.

This want of character in women manifests itself in the various enterprises which they undertake. We see it in literature, in the recklessness with which certain women steal illustrations, paragraphs, yea, whole lectures from one another, only being careful that the person stolen from should be sufficiently inconspicuous to prevent detection. It shows itself in unprincipled management of business. T. W. Hig-

ginson says, after setting forth the management of a young
woman on entering the lecture-field, "I have known something
of the lecture-field among men, for a good many years, and
I have seen some very underhand proceedings in connection
with it, but I felt that I, that every man who ever lectured
in America, must be pronounced a babe in innocence when I
saw the methods of this young woman." But has Mr. Higginson considered that this young woman has been taught nothing
of honor, dignity, or duty, except what is embraced in the
word "chastity"? Why expect anything but recklessness and
want of principle in other things? It is not the fault of woman's nature, but of bad education and false ideas, that such
want of principle as Mr. Higginson describes exists.

When one part of the nature is unduly stimulated, while
the rest left to slumber or die, the result is a dwarfed, un-
symmetrical character, a monstrosity from which the right
mind turns away with inexpressible pity. A good character
is composite in its nature, it is made up of a combination of
tastes, aspirations, virtues, gained by the experience of a
lifetime all bound together in one. A hundred tributary
streams unite to form the broad, even-flowing river. Coming down from the rugged peaks at the mountain top, a tiny
rill rushes over crags and ledges, over stones and brush-
wood, gathering new force with every inch of ground it trav-
erses; another, rising in some placid lake among the hills,
meandering through flowery vales, goes onward, bearing in
its waters the perfume of roses; some come from the east,
sparkling with the life and vivacity they have caught from the
winds that have swept over them; some from the west, tinged
with the hue of the fertile soils through which they have per-
colated. They all unite at last in the grand, majestic, mighty
river which carries refreshing moisture to the thirsty earth,
turns the mills of thrifty industry, bears upon its bosom giant
weights, lightening the labors of man, lending glory and beauty
to the landscape, until, scattering blessing along its whole
course, it mingles itself with the ocean.

So a noble character is formed, not of a single trick-
ling rill, pure and bright though it may be, but of many qualities combined. That energy which takes its rise among the
rough and rugged experiences of primitive society, and ever
presses on, gathering new life with every trial, that frugality
born of want, that integrity which is nurtured in the exact
world of business, that sweet charity begotten of a large
knowledge of human frailty, that gentle trustfulness acquired
by basking in the sunshine of Christian love--all these and

many more are the tributary streams which unite to form the noble Christian character; which shall be earnest and efficient in the work of the world, bearing the burdens of life without complaining itself a thing of beauty, lending blessedness to every scene until at last it mingles itself with that ocean of truth and love, the heart of God.

We seek for women the higher education which shall give them such a composite, many-sided, symmetrical Christian character; an education which shall give them the executive ability of the business man, the intellectual acumen of the scholar, the comprehensive thought of the philosopher, the prophetic vision of the seer, and all adorned and glorified by those Christian graces, faith, hope and charity.

It remains for us to consider the kind of education which will secure to women those qualities which most ennoble human character.

There are three sources of education--instruction, experience, and inspiration; and woman wants them all in their largest, fullest sense. She wants the best instruction which the age affords. Too long men have stingily doled out to us broken bits of knowledge, half-truths and make-believes. We have been fed these many years with crumbs from the rich man's table; it is time that we go home and sit with Abraham in the sunshine of eternal truth. If our colleges have been made repositories of the richest learning of the time, if there are garnered there the choicest stores of knowledge, the fullest libraries, the most complete cabinets, the most learned men, surely there woman ought to go and enrich herself by vast treasures of that knowledge which in all the ages of the past has made men wise and strong. Let her sit at the feet of the sages and refresh her mind with the knowledge of the wisest; let her hold converse with the poets and lift her soul into companionship with the purest spirits of all times. Let her accept no modified course, prepared with special reference to the female mind. Let her turn with contempt from the female seminary, that miserable farce with which women have been cheated by a semblance of learning without the reality, and demand all the instruction, in all departments of learning, that is given to men. Let the standard be fixed as high as may be, women must come up to the mark.

> Drink deep, or taste not the Pierean spring.
> There shallow draughts intoxicate the brain,
> And drinking largely sobers us again.

Does anybody tell us that these things are not possible
to woman, that her strength of body and power of mind are
insufficient to grasp the most profound subjects? I answer,
this is not a matter of speculation, it is a demonstrated fact
that women are capable both physically and mentally, of most
severe study and largest attainments. The names of illustri-
ous women, who in spite of the fetters imposed upon the sex,
have, in different periods of the world, achieved the highest
things in learning, rebuke the falsehood. The testimony of
the most experienced educators of our day, bears witness to
woman's ability. President Angell, of the Michigan Univer-
sity, says, "And I say with all frankness, that in all departments of study the young ladies have fully held their own, to
say the least, and no less in the higher mathematics than in
the departments of literature, they have shown the same variety of aptitude, the same variety of skill that the young men
have." In speaking of their physical endurance, he says,
"Any lady who can endure the draft that modern dress and
modern society make upon her, can certainly endure any college course so far as physical endurance is concerned. I am
simply here to bear testimony in the plainest way to what our
experience has shown. I have made it an object of particular
examination and scrutiny, and I am thoroughly convinced that
there is no danger which need be considered worthy of mention, for any young woman, in tolerably good health, in pursuing the regular course prescribed; nor has it actually been
the case that they have been impaired in health by the course."
Other testimonials might be brought to the same effect, although perhaps there is not other man of so high authority, who
has had the same opportunity to judge. But everyday experience is testing and revealing woman's ability, and with larger
opportunity her powers are being more fully demonstrated.
Why then should woman be content with partial courses of
study and superficial attainments? The whole world is her
own; there is no subject worthy the attention of mortals which
she may not study, no profound secret of nature which she
may not investigate, no height in the heavens to which she may
not aspire. As of old, wisdom was represented by goddess
Minerva, so still let woman's name stand for all that is excellent in learning. But the most complete and thorough instruction can avail little if it be not matured, assimilated,
and formed into character by the routine of daily experience.
Until then it is chaotic, formless and useless, like the red-
hot molten iron before it has been run in moulds or ham-
mered into useful implements.

Woman must from the streams of knowledge which

come seething from the brains of the wise, forge for herself
an armor in which to do battle with the world.   There can
be for her no great victories without conflict.   He is no true
soldier who expects to bear off the honors, while he sits on
cushioned chairs in luxurious parlors and simply reads books
of military tactics.   He only is worthy of the name of soldier, who has been the hero of a hundred fights, whose noble
scars bear witness of his valor on the field of battle, and
whose muscles have been trained to endurance by long and
perilous marches and the strict discipline of the camp.   So
woman must earn her title to valuable attainments, not by
merely memorizing bits of information, but by brave and
faithful service on the world's great battlefield.

Just that experience in the business of the world which
develops character in men, women need [in order] to make
them self-reliant, brave and true.   Says an eminent writer,
"A fine woman who has the qualities of a well-bred man is
the most agreeable of persons.   She combines the merit of
both sexes." And it is only by an experience in the great
world of business that woman's knowledge can be ripened,
and her character matured.   If boys after leaving school
went home to be supported and devoted themselves to needle-
work and novels, we should look for no noble manhood, and
only when girls cease to do this and seek some business of
life whereby to independently support themselves, and benefit
society, can we look for the truest womanhood.   But, says
some objector, women will no longer be angels when brought
in contact with the rude world.   Alas! the United States of
America in 1874 is not a favorable place for angels, nor are
the men of the nineteenth century suitable companions for
them.   An angel in American society at the present time
would be sadly out of place and very uncomfortable.   Even
that hymn by which little girls are made to sing,

I want to be an angel

adds,

And with the angels stand.

Nobody wants to be an angel and stand with unsuitable companions.   Since women are placed here in this very practical
and matter-of-fact world, it is well for them to make the
best of the situation, adapt themselves to the occasion, and
do the duty of the hour, and leave all angelic airs, until, by
a life of loving service of humanity, they shall have won for

themselves crowns brighter than those of angels. Since they
are surrounded by fallible, suffering mortals, let them give
themselves to the work of the world, that they may alleviate
the evils which they see about them, and in so doing, work
out their own salvation.

And this is the great argument in favor of the enfranchisement of women; it is not so much the repealing of wicked
laws, or the establishment of justice, although these are important, as it is that women should gain that self-respect and
independence which is the characteristic of the free. Not till
women share in the responsibilities and enjoy the privileges
of the enfranchised citizen can it be expected that they will
gain the highest excellence.

Freedom and responsibility have in all times been
thought essential conditions of mental growth in men; they are
not less essential to the development of women. Nor does
this larger life militate at all against those duties which are
peculiar to women. The position of wife and mother will be
far better filled by one whose mind is enlarged by a great
knowledge of affairs, and whose character is matured by the
discipline of life, than by one whose sympathies and whose
knowledge extends no farther than the half dozen or more
rooms which she calls her home.

It can be no possible advantage to a man that his
mother was socially a toy, financially a dependent, politically
a slave. On the contrary, the stream cannot rise higher than
its source, and if women are fettered, dependent, ignorant,
their sons will be narrow in mind, craven and cowardly.
When women are free and independent, and by experience in
the business of the world, shall have grown into the stature
of true womanhood, then, indeed, we may look for a race of
noble men such as the world has never seen. The larger
woman's experience is, the better is she fitted for every
duty, the more intelligently can she take any position to
which she is called.

And then woman wants the education of inspiration.
It is a grand thing to have a mind well stored with richest
learning, it is a better thing to have a character which has
been developed, strengthened and ripened by the actual experiences of life; but grander and higher than all, is the education which comes from communion with God. When the
soul comes to the throne of grace, and with earnest seeking,
looks to God for the truth, not content with a mere passing

wish or an aspiration but with intense prayer and longing it agonizes to enter into the realm of truth, then the will of the Lord is revealed, and his wondrous goodness is made known. Suddenly, sometimes, the soul beholds a vision of truth and beauty, the common daily task is transfigured, the world seems full of heavenly harmonies,

And every common bush afire with God.

Some call it intuition; the old prophets called it a vision. It is the Omnipotent deigning to answer the cry of the earnest soul. It is the education of inspiration. It is worth more than all the learning of the schools, more than all the discipline of a lifetime. It adds a new glory to all other knowledge.

But this education cannot come where vanity and folly hold sway. The small talk of society, the pretences and shams that make up so many women's lives, the excitements of the fashionable world, the trivial round of dress and gayety, all this is at war with the Holy Spirit, and cuts women off from this highest source of education. Rather let them retire, like the Master, to the mountain top or the wilderness, if only they may be alone with God. Some women fear to be alone, and wish to be always in society. For such there can be no high inspiration. It can only come in the solemn stillness, when the ear is closed to the gossip of the time, the opinions of men, the trifles of the world, and open only to the voice of God; when with terrible earnestness, the whole being yearns for the truth. The Infinite has no word for triflers or pretenders. To the sincere, earnest, questioning spirit alone is there given a response from on high. But that response, once heard, makes music in the soul forever; it purifies the heart, and ennobles character.

Let woman add to other attainments this communion with the Unseen, and they shall no longer desire that beauty which is merely of form and feature, for their countenances shall beam with a radiance from heaven; they shall walk the earth as angels of light; not such angels as require to be caged, shut up within four walls, kept out of useful business less they become contaminated, but angels "sent on embassies of mercy from an everlasting friend." When learning, experience and inspiration shall have combined to develop woman's character, then the objects of the higher education will have been attained, in the realization of the power and beauty of a true womanhood. We shall not see this ideal in our time--but we can work toward it.   Our standards of excellence, our educational institutions, our customs and laws should aim at the highest.   When the astronomer discovers a new planet, he first perceives by irregularities in the known, that there is an unknown body yet to be discerned. Then by careful computation, he estimates the place in the firmament where it ought to appear, determines its character, size and destiny.   Then stationed in his observatory, he watches through the long dark hours, night after night, corrects his estimates, and watches and waits again, until his patience is rewarded, and joy fills his heart as he beholds the heavenly body moving in its place, dispensing light and brilliancy along its pathway.   So the reformer who would seek the highest possibility of human nature, satisfied that we have not yet attained the best, considers the elements which make up a noble character, estimates the various influences which are necessary to produce such a character, modifies institutions, laws, customs, watches the results with untiring patience.   Years pass away, possibly generations, but at last, the world beholds that best, highest creation: a well-developed, symmetrical human character.

WOMEN AND SKEPTICISM
(January 25, 1885)

A Sermon Delivered at the Church of Our
Father, Washington, D.C. Phonetically
Reported by Miss Nettie White. Reprinted
in The Alpha, Vol. X, No. 7.

I have been informed that there was a sermon preached this
morning by Rev. Dr. Patton on Woman and Skepticism. I
cannot reply to Dr. Patton, because I did not hear him, but
I will preach a sermon from the same text he used--a part
of the Scripture lesson which has been read in your hearing.
It will be found in Luke xxiv:22, 23.

> Yea, and certain women also of our company made
> us astonished, which were early at the sepulchre.

> And when they found not His body, they came say-
> ing that they had also seen a vision of angels, which
> said that He was alive.

"Woman and Skepticism." I do not know why these
two words should be placed in connection, for it seems to me
that they are the very antipodes of each other. Skepticism
comes not by woman's sentiment, not by woman's spiritual
and affectionate nature, but comes more frequently from masculine logic. It comes more frequently from the profound
metaphysics of the learned doctors. It is written: "The pure
in heart shall see God." I do not find any place in the Scriptures wherein heaven or heavenly things, or any revelation of
Divine truths, are promised to metaphysicians or the learned
doctors. It is written: "The pure in heart shall see God."
I do not find any place in the Scriptures wherein heaven or
heavenly things, or any revelation of Divine truths, are promises unto those whose hearts are open to sympathy and tenderness, and so I believe that even according to the conde-
scensions of the sterner sex, women may reasonably expect
to have at least their share of a knowledge of God, which is
called theology. It is notorious, I think, that women have

taken especial interest in religion everywhere the world over,
and in all ages.   In our own times you know that the largest
part of almost all the congregations of the country are made
up of women.   You know that the Sabbath-school and the
prayer-meeting and the conference meeting would be impos-
sibilities without woman's cooperation, woman's devotion,
and woman's self-sacrifice.   You know that in a great many
churches over this broad land of ours it is woman's faithful
labor, woman's sacrifice, that enables the church treasury
to do its work and the minister's salary to be paid.   And
not confining ourselves to our own country, if we go abroad
to other lands, if we look beyond the Christian religion even,
we shall find everywhere that the spirit of religion has seemed
to characterize woman.   It is recognized all through the Bi-
ble--woman's peculiar fitness and adaptation to the great interests of the soul.   And when, in the beginning, according
to the grand revelation that we have there of the beginning
of things, when God called things into being, He made this
human race, "male and female created he them"--not him.
He gave them dominion over the fish of the sea, over the
fowls of the air, and over every creeping thing on the face
of the earth; all the wealth of this world, all that it can
yield, all the vast resources of this earth, were given equally
to woman and to man.   And then, in the fullness of time,
Jesus Christ came to the world and revealed himself peculiarly to women.   It was a mother's insight, a mother's devotion, a mother's spiritual nature, that so enabled her to
hear the voices of the angels and to recognize that the Savior
of the world was to be born; and in those long months of
watching and pondering all these things in her heart, the angels came very near to her, and the Divine Spirit was so
rested upon her that when Christ came to the world he came
with a woman's tenderness in His nature, and woman's spiritual perception, with a woman's great sympathy for fallen,
suffering, downtrodden humanity everywhere, and He revealed
Himself first of all to woman.   It was in obedience to a
mother's command that He left the temple, where He was
sitting with the doctors asking them questions and hearing
of the grand mysteries of the universe.   Obedient unto a
mother's command, He went out of the temple, and went to
the humble home; and in learning truths from the association
with this mother through the first thirty years of his life, He
was prepared for the grand work to which He was called; and
then, when the time came that He should declare His mission
He did not seek out the learned scribes and leaders of the
church; he did not present Himself to the rabbis, the doctors
of divinity of that day, and present them with certain logical

deductions. O, no! He met the sinful and sorrowing woman
at the well--the woman whom the world derided, the woman
that belonged to the sect that the Jews hated--and he there
declared Himself to her as the Messiah. He bade her go
forth and proclaim that the Messiah had come. He performed
His first miracle at the command of a woman. It was women
who were His intimate friends and companions and to whom
He spoke of the great mysteries that He came to declare;
and when in the last trying hour men proved cowardly and
faithless, when they ran away, or followed Him only at a
distance; when Peter denied His Lord, and one of His followers had betrayed Him, women stood faithfully at the foot
of the cross, and with tender and weeping hearts looked on
while the suffering Lord, looking upon them in pity and in
love, ascended up to God. And when the disciples, discovering the disappearance concerning the fulfillment of the
prophecies, ran away, not knowing what to do, it was women
who came early in the morning to the sepulchre, and it was
they who saw the vision of the angels and knew that the Lord
had risen. To them He spoke, and said: "Why weepest thou?
Go and tell My disciples that I am risen from the dead."

We read that women, for a long time shut out of the
churches and standing in the outer courts of the synagogue,
not recognized as having souls, scarcely admitted to any of
the privileges of men, were first welcomed to the gatherings
of early Christians, and were invited to bear their testimony.
There they told the story of their joys and hopes.

That grand old hero, the Apostle Paul, vindicated the
rights of women, sending them out to do his work and to
preach the gospel, preparing them to be effectual laborers
in the cause of Christ, giving them kindly, friendly advice
as to the manner in which they should deport themselves;
that they should not appear with uncovered heads when they
proclaimed the prophecy--for that word in the New Testament
does not mean the foretelling of future events, but elevated
or instructive discourse. "When your women prophesy let it
be with their heads covered." So careful was this earnest
laborer in the cause of Christ in regard to the reputation of
these women, so careful lest they should do something which
might bring upon them a misjudgment of society, that he gave
them advice even as to their wearing apparel, welcoming them
to the good work to which Christianity had opened the door.
But you may say, perhaps, if Christ, and if the apostles, if
Christianity opens the door of opportunity to women and in-
vites them to this large liberty, how does it happen that the

Christian churches through these many years have failed to
recognize their preaching and have kept women out of the pulpit, and out of all the opportunities for laboring publicly for
the upbuilding of truth in the world?

The reader of ecclesiastical history goes back to the
early centuries, follows the course of the church through the
first one or two centuries, and notes how, by degrees, Christianity became mingled with the fallacies of surrounding religions, how little by little it fell away from its original purity. The reader of the history of the early Christian church
recalls the time when it was patronized by the authority of the
State, when it became a State religion, when it took upon it
ceremonials, expensive pomps and shows and departed from
its original simplicity in form and manner of devotion. And
you recollect that at that time there came in this horrible
doctrine of the depravity of woman, and the immorality of
women. The pollution attendant upon her touch was such that
holy men, who would know of the things of God, ministers of
Christ who would proclaim the gospel of the world's salvation,
must not even be associated with women. And then came in
the celibacy of the clergy. How, consequent upon that, and
following immediately upon it, there came in such a reign of
iniquity to the Christian church, such a lowering down of the
whole moral standard, such depraving of the morals of the
entire community, that it prepared the way for the dark ages
that settled down upon Europe, in which the moral nature of
man seemed to be slumbering in one long lethargy approxi-
mating unto death. It was only when Luther, recognizing the
right of man to free thought and independent action, dealt the
deathblow not only to the sale of indulgences, but to the supremacy of the pope and the celibacy of the clergy as well.
It was only when Luther took that stand that the world began
to rise and man began to come out into the light and liberty
of God's children. Slowly through the ages since that time
our church, the church of Christ, has been coming nearer to
the original ideal of primitive Christianity, but it has taken
centuries to outgrow that false teaching and those evil customs; so we have had handed down along the ages the doctrine that women were not to speak in the church on doctrines; that women were not to be known in the councils of
the State; that they were to have no part in the affairs of the
nation, but they must be continually under bonds, subject unto
masters, living entirely with their sympathies shut within the
four walls of home, knowing no broader interest than those
of their own family, and no higher aims than the material
wants of food and clothing, doing nothing grander nor better

for their children than merely to attend to their physical ne-
cessities.

We are told that liberty for women leads to skepticism; that it leads to immorality, that it leads to infidelity
in marriage.   The facts of history will bear me witness that
such as not been found to be the effect of liberty in men.
We have seen what liberty has done for men.   No republican,
no American who believes in our republican institutions but
will grant that it is only in the atmosphere of liberty that noble characters can be developed; that it is the free man whom
the truth makes free, and that while a man is hedged in and
shut down he cannot attain to his best.   If you compare the
people belonging to the laboring community in our own country with those who come over to us from the old world, bearing in their characters and on their faces the marks of years
of servitude; if you compare them, I say, with the noble me-
chanics, farmers, laboring men of all classes of our own
country, you will see the difference between liberty and servitude; and you will recognize that it is only in an atmosphere
of liberty that the human race reaches its grandest complete-
ness.   It is under the influence of religious institutions, where
men are held responsible for their conduct, where they have
high aims, where honorable remuneration is afforded, and
where they have within their grasp the opportunities of the
world, that men grow strong, heroic, self-reliant, and in all
respects worthy to be called the children of God.

Now if liberty does all this for men, if it makes them
true and brave and strong, self-reliant and earnest, why
should it not have the same effect upon women?   What reason can be given why freedom for women should lead to skepticism, why freedom for women should lead to immorality.
I have not the time tonight--and perhaps this is not the proper
place--to vindicate the characters of those women whom I understand were slandered by Dr. Patton this morning.   Had I
the time, I believe I could show you that the noble character
of Madam Roland makes a bright spot on one of the darkest
pages of European history.   Had I the time I might possibly
show you that Frances Wright, although charged by many with
heresy, was never charged by any man on the face of the
earth with any departure from principles of morality and purity.   I might show you, perhaps, that even poor Woodhull--
sinful, wandering, visionary, filled with error, mistaken, betrayed, branded--is still a human being, still a child of the
dear Father, having in her no doubt aspirations for something
better; longing for the higher life, and desiring to enter into

the light and liberty of the children of God; but hedged in and
fettered, this part of her higher nature has been perverted
and turned aside.   I might possibly show you these things had
I time, but time does not permit.   Rather let me call your
attention to the long line of noble women whose beautiful characters make American history grand and inspiring, the noble
women who, under the influence and inspiration of republican
institutions, and within the limits of the Christian church,
have done honor to American womanhood.

      Let me call to your minds the noble women of the
Revolution, who were willing to peril their lives and give all
for their country, for liberty, and at the same time were the
most devoted of Christians.   Let me remind you of Mrs. Ad-
ams, so noble that when the great statesman, her son, at his
height of power, referred to her, he said: "All that I am I
owe to my mother."   Let me remind you of the noble women
who, during the war of the rebellion, left their homes here
in the North and went down upon battlefields that they might
minister to the suffering and dying.

      Let me remind you of Lucretia Mott, a woman as it
seems to me of the most beautiful character that has yet been
presented before the world, in this our country; a woman so
Christ-like, so trusting, so devoted, that everybody who came
within the reach of her influence was baptized with the Holy
Spirit.   She, let me remind you, was the founder of the National Woman Suffrage Association, and for forty years its
representative before the people, holding during her lifetime
an important office in that association.   I do not know why
the reverend doctor forgot to mention Mrs. Mott in the array
of women that he presented to his audience.   I am told that
it was not for want of having her picture at his side, as it
had been presented to him very recently.   But such a woman,
a representative of those who advocate a larger liberty for
all women, a representative of the Christian church, a woman
reared in the atmosphere of the larger liberty which the Society of Friends extend to women--such a woman is a complete refutation of the charge that freedom for women leads
to skepticism or to immorality.   We are told that freedom
for women means infidelity in the marriage relation and leads
to the frequency of divorce; but let me remind you, my brothers, that as yet the women of this land have had no voice in
making the laws on the subject of divorce.   If you have lax
laws on that subject, if they admit of more divorces than are
warranted by the doctrines of the Christian religion, it is not
the fault of women.   No law on the subject of divorce has

been made by women, or has been made in response to any
petition coming up from women. No such law has been asked
for by the women of the land. If they are wrong--and this
is not the place to discuss that subject--the burden of responsibility rests upon those men who have taken it upon
themselves to make all the laws upon this and every other
subject. Until the women of this land have had some voice
in legislation on the subject of marriage and divorce, it is
not fitting that any class of women shall be held chargeable
with the wrong that is done in those laws.

Freedom for women, we are told, leads to immorality.
On the contrary, look around you. What is acknowledged to
be the great primary cause of the licentiousness, of the immorality of the time? Is it that women are so self-sustaining,
so independent, so strong, so capable in regard to their financial relations of self-support? O, no! The story of the
prostitute is, in two-thirds of the cases, I think I am safe in
saying, a story of want, a story of poverty, a story of ignorance, a story of betrayal because of her weakness and her
dependence. The first cause of the immorality of the time
is that women have been hampered, that they have been kept
down, that they have been kept poor, until they become the
easy victims of licentious men; and while men hold the power
in their hands, and while they hold all the remunerative employments for themselves, while they have charge of the
wealth of this nation and remand women to places where they
get a miserable pittance that only keeps body and soul together, let no man on this earth charge upon women the immorality of the time. The immoralities of this day grow out
of the subordination of women, and the great remedy must
come by making women self-sustaining and financially independent. Sometimes when I look around me and realize how
licentiousness is increasing in this land, how it is spreading
itself far and wide, contaminating all classes of society with
its slimy touch; when I realize how, with the larger wealth
that is coming to our people, the door is opened to self-
indulgence, when I see how intemperance is carrying our
bravest and noblest and most beautiful young men down to
shameful deaths, or on to lives of degradation and misery;
when I realize all this, I stand fearful concerning the future.
I look anxiously on, and ask, what next?

In this grand city of yours, as I go up and down the
broad streets and see the grand buildings that rear themselves
on every hand; as I note the beauty of your Capitol, with its
perfect symmetry, its works of art, its beautiful fresco work

and its pictures; when I look at all these public buildings and
institutions, as they lift their grand proportions before men,
standing forth as the symbol of prosperity and of the wealth
and the growth of this nation; when I look around me here in
Washington and see people gathered from all parts of this
great Union, from the Atlantic to the Pacific, from the North
and the South, all along the line representing varieties of industry, the thousands of forms of activity that are going forward here, I say: Can it be that this great free nation is
destined to go out and to be known no more on the face of
the earth, as has happened to nations of the Old World? And
then I look at our Declaration of Independence, our Constitution of the United States, and it seems to me that such principles ought to live, that the Union of the people and for the
people, and a government by the people ought to stand; and
when I see the multitudes from the Old World fleeing from
tyranny and from poverty, and oppression in its various
forms, coming here to find homes, I say, it seems to me
that this nation shall live.   And yet, over on the other side,
where those great crimes that have been the cause of the
downfall of all the nations of the world--immorality, self-
indulgence, impurity, licentiousness, intemperance--these
things have sapped the foundations of the proudest nations of
the Old World.   They have brought the most powerful governments to ruin; they have laid low the mightiest cities, and
they have weakened the strongest peoples; and they will do
the same for us, unless we can find somewhere a reserve
force in our community that shall rise up and infuse into our
political and social life an element of faith, or charity, of
purity, and of hope.   Unless we can bring the womanhood of
America to take part in the councils of the nation, to take
their part in the instruction given to the people by means of
the pulpit, the platform, and the press; unless we can have
woman's faith and hope, woman with her vision of the angels
to make the world pure and strong and good; unless we can
have these we shall go out in darkness, as other nations have
done before us.

        I have said that women were by nature and by the pe-
culiarities of their circumstances and experiences fitted for
religious impression.   It is woman's peculiar experience that
enables her to receive the vision of the angels.   It is in the
long months when she recognizes that the responsibility is
resting upon her of forming the character of the new being
that is to come to the earth; it is through that long period,
with trustful, hopeful watching and prayer, she feels the min-
istration of the immortalities and the Divine Spirit closes

around her and there come to her revelations of truth and
duty which no man in all this world ever can experience.
Then she sees with the eye of faith beyond the things of this
present time.   She looks above things that are seen and passing, recognizing the things that are unseen and everlasting.
God speaks to her soul and she feels the Divine presence.
Let us have the mothers of the land, with their high inspiration and the songs of the angels resounding in their ears, the
dear Christ bending over them in loving sympathy.   Let us
have them in the councils of the State and in the places of
influence, and let them translate the songs of the angels into
human laws and incarnate them in human institutions, that
there may be a high and pure moral standard placed before
all the people; that we may rise out of our materialism and
our sensualism to live for the highest aims, to aspire to realize here on the earth that kingdom which is peace and
righteousness and joy in the Holy Ghost.

    I said to you that I am filled with anxiety with re-
gard to our future, that my heart stands still sometimes when
I realize the sin and sorrow that is around me, and yet I am
not hopeless concerning our future.   I see evidence of growth
and I see the evidence of enlargement of intellectual vision
all around me.   It is a significant omen of our times, and
one of the grandest omens, too, that all the colleges worth
speaking of, with one or two insignificant exceptions like those
of Harvard and Tufts (I do not know that I should expect Harvard since it has an annex for women), have opened their
doors and welcomed women.   Not only that, but almost all
the presidents of the colleges have borne testimony that women
have acquitted themselves as nobly in learning their lessons,
and they have appeared in the recitation rooms as regularly,
and have graduated with as high honors as their masculine
companions in the same classes.   It is one of the grandest
omens of our time that Dr. Patton himself is at the head of
an institution where men and women are educated upon equal
terms.   He signs the diplomas that shall recommend them to
the world as educated in the arts and sciences and letters
necessary to make them useful citizens of the Republic.   It
is a grand omen of the times that the church is outgrowing
the darkness of the Middle Ages and getting back to the teachings of Christ and the Apostle Paul, and is sending women
out as Paul did, to labor in the Lord, and I thank God that
my own church, the Universalist, has been the one to open
the door of opportunity to women who wish to proclaim the
glad tidings of the whole world's salvation, and that thirty
women (I think it is nearer forty by this time) have come

forward to enter into the work, and to obey the command that
Christ gave to those women who were last at the cross and
first at the sepulchre, to go abroad "tell the disciples that
I am risen from the dead." It is a grand omen of our time
that while this morning one reverend doctor was preaching
against liberty for women and held up to the scorn of the
congregation some unfortunate women, and some grand women
that he slandered, another minister in another church--I think
it was the Calvary (some good church of Christ)--was bearing
testimony to the beauty of woman's character, to the effi-
ciency of her work, and to the recognition that Christianity
gives to woman's fitness for public work. So, I say we are
not without hope. Many of the churches are recognizing
woman's capability for usefulness. Some of the States have
recognized that she is capable of judging of a school committee, while Wyoming and Washington have given her the
ballot.

The time is pregnant with hope; let us not despair,
but let us listen for the voices of the angels. Today, as of
old, He speaks to sorrowing, downtrodden and oppressed
woman, and now, as then, He says: "Woman, why weepest
thou? Go tell my disciples that I am risen from the dead."
Christ is risen: He rises today, let us shake off the grave
clothes that have hung about our race through the ages of the
past; let us rise out of that lethargy, and put on new life that
is with Christ in God; and, brothers and sister, let us walk
forth together in the light and liberty of the children of God.

Address Delivered at the Rockford Fair
Reported in the Rockford (Ill.) Star

The prosperity of a nation depends on the patriotism of the
people. When patriotism declines, national hope declines;
we need to revive our love of country by dwelling often on
what our liberties have cost. We must place ourselves with
the Pilgrim Fathers, when leaving comfortable homes in the
old world they faced danger, sickness and death in the wilderness, that they might lay the foundation to our free republic. We should go with Arnold in that journey to Quebec.
We should go with mad Anthony Wayne as he faced shot and
shell at the storming of Stony Point.

We should starve with Washington at Valley Forge, we
should follow the bloody trail of the soldiers of the revolution
as they marched through winter snows, and then, perhaps,
we can form some faint ideas of what our liberties have cost.
Yet all this is a small part of the strife and struggle of the
sorrow and tears by which liberty for our race has been
achieved. Nations have travailed together in pain until now
that a free republic might be born on this western continent.
And these free institutions are represented by the ballot.

The ballot is the inheritance we have received from
all the ages of the past. It stands for centuries of trial, the
prayers and tears of the toiling multitudes, as one by one
they have broken old fetters, torn down old tyrannies, and
step by step achieved the emancipation of our race. It is
a right which has been reaped from fields of suffering and
blood. It represents the grandeur of history and all the highest hopes of humanity.

None but cowards and fools speak lightly of the value
of the ballot. The historian knows full well at what great
price this right was purchased. The philosopher sees in the
ballot the guardian of liberty, the protection of individual,

109

personal and property rights, the avenue to honor and emolument, the great educator of the people, the security of everything that humanity holds dear. By means of it, labor has been elevated, the laborer has been enabled to secure fair play in the conflicts of the world and to make an honorable position for himself and his children.

[The speaker sketched rapidly the history of labor, showing what the ballot has done for the laboring man. She contrasted the condition of our laborers with the disfranchised men of other countries, showing that the ballot awakened honorable ambition, opened doors of opportunity and elevated the condition of the laboring man. She continued,] Woman needs the incentives and protections which the ballot gives. No slave on southern plantation was ever in a worse condition than the slave girls of our great cities. Nowhere is humanity so outraged and justice so far forgotten as in those dens of infamy to which women are too often driven by want. As we read these terrible records, we see that woman needs the ballot for protection. What the ballot has done for men, in elevating labor and securing better conditions, it will do for women.

Men's wages are higher than women's, even in the same departments. Woman needs the ballot for the same reasons that man needs it. She wants it as an educator. If girls are now not posted on politics it is because the knowledge is something they have never expected to use. But give them the ballot, and it will be an incentive to study. Woman needs the ballot as a protection from injustice in the work of the world. The reason why women are underpaid and their work undervalued is not because they are women, but because they are disfranchised. Disfranchised classes the world over are hampered in their industries and cheated in their wages. Why should women be disfranchised in a republic which boasts to all the world that it offers freedom and equality to all its citizens? Women have made this country what it is. They have borne their part bravely in its wars, often fighting in the ranks till the war was ended and they were honorably mustered out of service. As pioneers in this western world they have helped to develop the country; they have cultivated the soil, working outdoors and indoors; they have been loyal to the government, and by their intelligence and character contributed to upholding the commonwealth. Yet they are made politically the subjects of tramps, paupers, drunkards, ignorant men of every nation on the face of the globe. It can no longer be said that they do not know enough to vote.

Two-thirds of the graduates of our colleges are women.
Four-fifths of our school teachers are women.   One hundred
thousand chautauquans are women.   Women are studying all
kinds of subjects in their homes.   Woman represents education today.   She represents religion.   The great majority of
the Protestant church members are women.

We enfranchise the saloon and the poorhouse, the irresponsible classes.   We disfranchise the home, the church,
the school.   We make the daughters of America subject to the
serfs and slaves from the old world.   Such policy is suici-
dal.   The aristocracies of the old world are based upon noble
birth, superior qualifications, merit in some form.   The subject classes in the old world are the lower and more ignorant
classes.   America alone presents the spectacle of an aristocracy of pantaloons.   We are the first people to try the
experiment of enfranchsing ignorance, drunkenness and all
forms of vice, and subordinating intelligence, patriotism, religion.   Such an experiment must fail.   Already our republican institutions are in peril, with the great preponderance of
foreign voters, the conflict of varied interests, the great gulf
fixed between capital and labor, our republic is on the verge
of ruin.   The only hope of the nation is in the enfranchisement of woman.   The census shows us the American women
greatly outnumber American men.   Among the foreign-born
the men outnumber the women.   The voting of women means
a vote for American institutions, for a free government, a
free church, a vote for purity, temperance and home.   Every
great interest is in peril until women vote.   If there is a
man here who loves his country he should do his utmost for
the enfranchisement of women.

If women love home or children or believe in purity
or desire the establishment of virtue, let them seek the right
of suffrage with might, mind, and strength.   The emergency
is pressing.   Our dangers are great.   The time for work is
now.   Let each one do with her might what her hand findeth
to do in this great work.

Address Given Before the National American
Woman Suffrage Convention
Printed in The Woman's Tribune, March 8, 1890

In the call which was issued for this convention, attention
was called to the fact that we are now in the midst of a series of centennial celebrations marking the great progress
which our race has made--that our country and our people
have made--during the last hundred years. It is a significant fact that at the very time when we are rejoicing over
the progress made, when we are congratulating ourselves
most over what we have done, when we are celebrating the
work achieved by those who have gone before--at the very
moment, there seems to be on all sides a general confession that, after all, it has all been a mistake. Just when
we stand at the mountain top of a hundred years of almost
unexampled prosperity and progress we find statesmen and
eminent writers, and even the common people on every hand,
ready to deny the very foundation principles on which our
Government is based, and through which we have come up
to our present prosperity. An eminent writer during the
past year has announced that the great fundamental principle
on which this Government is based, the right of all the people to voice in the Government by which they are controlled--
that is, that suffrage is an inherent right--is "rubbish left
over from the philosophers of the eighteenth century"; and
we hear it said that "it is a great mistake that we have extended the suffrage as we have done"; "a great mistake to
have enfranchised the Negro"; a great mistake to have welcomed people here from all parts of the world and to have
extended the right of suffrage to so many of them, as we
have done. Men seem ready to deny the very fundamental
laws upon which the Government rests, and therefore when
we come down here to Washington it is not, as in former
years, to take our stand on the Constitution of the United
States and the Declaration of Independence, and there ask
for woman's suffrage, but we must go back and reconsider

those things which were supposed to be acknowledged by all,
to inquire whether this Government is, after all, a mistake.

The first great principle on which our Government
rests--the inherent right of suffrage--namely, that all are
created free and entitled alike to life, liberty and the pursuit of happiness, is not rubbish left over from the philosophers of the eighteenth century, for it goes back, clear back,
to the apostle Paul, when he announced that God created of
"one blood all the nations of the earth"--back to the time
when the great Master proclaimed that it was "neither at
this mountain nor yet at Jerusalem that men should worship
the Father," thus breaking down all barriers between clique
and class and clan, and recognizing that all are one. This
is no rubbish, but the eternal gospel, God's living truth.

Another principle, that taxation and representation
must, where justice reigns, go together--that they are in-
separable--this is no rubbish left over from the eighteenth
century. No; it is a principle that has been dear to the
hearts of Englishmen for six hundred years, running back
to the time when Edward I proclaimed that there should be
a representation of boroughs in Parliament; not that he was
a philanthropist or a reformer and wished to extend the rights
of the people, but because he was sharp enough to perceive
that he could get more money by calling the people together
to vote money than by taking it by force, and hence he insti-
tuted this representation of boroughs.

You have also heard that it was natural for men to
vote. People speak often as though a ballot-box was the very
first thing a male infant cried for; whereas the rattle comes
before, and many of them do not get out of the rattle-box
stage all their lives; and so it came about when these men
of England were called to sit in Parliament and take part in
the councils of the realm, they did not want to vote; they
wanted to stay comfortably at home and let the clergy and
the lords and the king manage the government. They had
all the rights they wanted. They were very much like the
women of today; but after six hundred years of trial, that
principle that there is no right by which any government can
impose taxes without a representation of those upon whom
those taxes are imposed--that principle, once received into
the hearts of Englishmen, has been held precious wherever
the English people have gone; that is not rubbish of the last
century; that is a principle that will stand forever, as long
as there is a universe or a God to reign over that universe.
That is no mistake.

It is a mistake, they say, to enfranchise the Negro.
If it is a mistake, then the Republican party, in every utter-
ance that it has ever made, is a mistake; then the Government is a mistake, and the Declaration of Independence is a
mistake; the Constitution of the United States is a mistake,
and the Christian religion is a mistake; Edward I is a mistake, and history is a mistake. No race, no nation, I will
venture to say, in twenty-five years has ever made the progress that the colored people have made in that time. To
liberate four millions of men out of ignorance and degradation, and to raise them into self-respecting citizens, into intelligence and the power of earning an honest living, and doing their part of the world's work, is not a mistake. But it
is said to be a mistake to have invited foreigners here as
we have done; to have all the people of the world coming
here and sharing our inheritance. I ask, what could we have
done without these foreigners? The Irishmen have tunneled
our mountains, and drained our marshes, and built our railroads; the Germans have cultivated the broad fields, and made
the desert blossom as the rose; the Welshmen have filled the
land with melody, as they sang their sweet songs and lifted
up their voices in devotion. Every nationality has done something. We have learned something from them all, and all
have contributed to the strength and the glory of our great
country. They have helped us to subdue and to extend our
dominion from ocean to ocean. It is not a mistake to have
invited them here. Had we pursued a narrow, exclusive policy, we might have today been a little, conceited, bigoted,
narrow-minded band of colonies, crawling along the shores
of the Atlantic, instead of this great people, reaching from
ocean to ocean, and possessing the entire continent. They
have all done their part. Where, then, is the mistake? For
everybody says there is a mistake, and evidently there is
one; for have we not dissatisfaction on every side; have we
not contention and a great gulf yawning between capital and
labor--one class arrayed against another class; and have we
not in our cities the danger presented to us that the red flag
of anarchy and revolution will be raised in our midst; and
have we not continual reports that there is deceit and bull-
dozing, and bribery, and riots, and even murders, on every
side? Have we come, then, to a condition of peace? No,
there is a mistake--a serious mistake. Where is it? There
is a mistake always when any man is unjust to his neighbor--
when he cheats his neighbor--and a greater mistake when he
cheats himself. That man who cheats his neighbor is guilty
of dishonesty and folly; but the man who cheats himself is as
dishonest as the one who cheats his neighbor, and a hundred
fold more stupid.

Now, the native American man is all the time cheating himself; he cheats himself when he takes away the ballot from his wife and mother and sister, and at the same time gives it to every man that lands on our shore, whether he be pauper, tramp, drunkard, or what not; he cheats himself when he gives the ballot to a foreign people and disfranchises those of his own family.

Mr. Ingalls said, in his recent speech, that "there is nothing so unprofitable as injustice" and I think that the sentiment is true. What can be more unprofitable to the men of this nation than to cheat their wives out of the ballot and thus allow themselves to be governed by a minority of foreigners? How unprofitable to the American men of Wisconsin to allow a million of native-born people to be governed by four or five hundred thousand foreigners. How unprofitable and unwise and stupid that all the American men allow themselves to be outvoted and governed by a small minority of foreigners, and this they do by the disfranchisement of women, giving the ballot to all classes of men and denying it to their own household. We see that these foreigners are much more largely masculine than feminine, as men, from various causes, emigrate to this country more largely than women; some emigrate to escape from justice, or because they are able to get away with greater convenience, or for some reason or other. We see that seven men come to this country to one woman; while at the same time the native-born men have been killed in the war, some by accident, and some have killed themselves by the use of tobacco and rum. Thus native-born men sell themselves into bondage to foreigners by the disfranchisement of women. Isn't that a mistake?

What an awful mistake has been committed in the South, where, when the war was ended and great numbers of white men had been killed off, the ballot was put into the hands of colored men, and all those white people, of which the greater part were women, were given into bondage, if you please, to those who but recently had been their slaves. It was simply giving the white population of the South into the hands of the Negro to be governed by them. I have in my possession a most pathetic letter from a good, cultured, noble woman of Mississippi, in which she describes the situation there--how the sheriff and the treasurer and the clerk of the county where she lives are colored men; and it so happened in this instance that these three officers were men who had formerly been her slaves, and who could not read nor write; and she says: "You Northern women wouldn't like it"; and you all know that you wouldn't like it, and there is

nothing so unprofitable as injustice.   As Senator Ingalls has
said, "God is the most relentless of creditors."   And there
will be bloodshed as long as this continues and our Southern
sisters are thus trespassed upon.   I don't wonder that those
people of the South are dissatisfied.   You would be, in the
same position.   You know it full well.   Not that I would take
the ballot from the Negro, but I would put the ballot in the
hands of the women of the South, that they may defend themselves and outvote the colored race.   You may kill a man by
outvoting him, and it is a great deal easier and pleasanter
than by dynamite or even by electricity.   But I would take
the ballot from no man; they have just the same right to vote
that I have, and I have just the same right that any man on
the earth has.   But let us have justice--that "justice" which
Senator Ingalls says "is the universal solvent of all human
difficulties, for which every place should be a temple, and
all seasons summer."   That is fine.   I wish that Senator Ingalls knew something about it, but I am afraid that he doesn't.
Is justice only to be extended to those who have strong weapons of warfare in their hands, and know pretty well how to
use them?   I am afraid that he has not thought of a people
who cannot or will not wage carnal warfare for their rights.

There was an injustice when the women of Utah were
disfranchised, but I never heard of Senator Ingalls lifting up
his voice, to say that "justice is the universal solvent of all
human difficulties, and for which every place should be a
temple, and all seasons summer."

There was a terrible injustice wrought when the women
of Washington Territory were disfranchised, but I never heard
of Senator Ingalls saying one word about the unprofitableness
of injustice, and that God was the most relentless of all creditors; yet those sentiments were just as true then, in that
application, as they are now, or can be in any application.
The principles of justice are just as inexorable when applied
to people who have no guns or bayonets, as they are when
applied to an armed soldiery, and God will have his vengeance
just as surely upon the wrong done to the weakest of his children as though it had been done to the United States army
with weapons in their hands; that is a lesson I do not believe
that Senator Ingalls has learned.

Mr. Blackwell gave you a few figures last night, but
he didn't give you half enough of them.   He might have told
you that in North Carolina there are 173,000 more white
women than colored women, and that if women were enfran-

chised in North Carolina it would give the white race a larger
vote than that of the colored race; he might have told you that
the figures in all the Southern states, with the exception of
Mississippi and South Carolina, show full plainly that if women
were enfranchised it would immediately give the balance of
power to the white race; that he could kill the Negro by kind-
ness--by out-voting him.   He might have told you that in South
Carolina the enfranchisement of all women, upon a reading
and writing basis, would give a white vote of 161, 000 and a
colored vote of only 107, 000, in round numbers; he might
have told you that in Mississippi, the banner state for color,
the enfranchisement of women, upon a reading and writing
basis, would give a white vote of 164, 000, in round numbers,
and a colored vote of only 153, 000; thus even in Mississippi,
giving the whites an advantage of over ten thousand votes.
Does not that show that the enfranchisement of women would
settle the vexed question at the South without exporting anybody or killing anybody?   Does it not show at once that justice is the universal solvent for solving all human difficulties?   I am grateful to Mr. Ingalls for the sentiment, for it
is a noble one, and I hope you will all take it home with you
and remember that "justice is the universal solvent that will
solve all human difficulties. "

And Mr. Blackwell might have given you more figures
still; he might have told you that the figures furnished by the
chief of the bureau of statistics in Massachusetts show that
in Massachusetts the native born women would out-vote the
whole foreign population and 2, 000, 000 votes besides.   Everybody knows that those Massachusetts women have views, and
we want those women to express their views at the ballot box.
He might have told you, if he had chosen, that he had the
figures which show conclusively that not only in Massachusetts, but in other states and in the various great cities of
our land, the enfranchisement of women is only necessary to
vote down the whole foreign population, and make secure our
free Government, free church, and our quiet homes; and who
is there that does not desire these things?

But, oh! women tell me, it is all true, and they want
the ballot, but they are so much occupied with other things.
They are doing church work; working in the philanthropic societies, and doing something for the poor, and working for
this and that society, and contriving more healthful articles
of head-gear and foot-gear and hand-gear, and they are doing
more--they are organizing to put God into the Constitution,
and some of them to keep him out; but, friends, you can do

nothing for God or humanity with your hands tied. The first
thing is to free yourselves from this bondage in order to help
some good cause. When you present your petitions to legislative bodies they will not notice you. They laugh at the
sweet simplicity of these dear women who come with their
petitions, when they know they have not a particle of power.

Men tell us that we are responsible for the home and
the education of the children; that the morals of society are
in our keeping. Why, how absurd that is! Suppose, when
the war was raging, our generals had taken some of those
tall, stalwart men and bound their hands behind and put them
in the front, and told them to go in and win--what would have
happened? Evidently the army would have been cut to pieces,
and they would have been entirely routed; but that is what the
men are doing with us; they put us in the front of the great
battle that is waging against intemperance, gambling, impurity, and they take away the only weapon which anybody could
use in a republic and they say they expect you to keep the
peace, and hold you responsible for the morals of the community. Our first business is to free ourselves from this
bondage before we can help any cause, and then, when we
are free, we shall not go about getting up strawberry festi-
vals, and oyster suppers, and crazy quilt lotteries, but we
shall vote appropriations. At present, women are utterly
powerless with regard to the great evils which they are asked
to overcome, and the first service we can render to the
church or to the anti-church--the first service that we can
render to humanity or to God, is to get ourselves into a position of independence.

My heart has been pained here at this convention as
there have come to me reports from ladies from different
states represented, telling me of horrible wrong and outrage
that is done to the insane and the unfortunate pauper in alms-
houses and eleemosynary institutions, and they come and ask
us to do something about it; and one woman said to me, as
she told of this: "I see that you don't mean to do anything
about it." It is a bad thing, but what can we do about it,
women? We have no power. We are petitioners and pen-
sioners upon the bounty of men ourselves. They say we
ought to work in these directions. Every one of the officers
of these charities, these guardians of the poor, whatever offices they may hold, these physicians and attendants of the
insane asylums, hold their places as a reward for services
done to some political party. Every one is entitled to a place
because he has voted Harrison up or Cleveland out, or some-

thing of that sort. If we have ballots, then we can remove
these offensive members, and put woman in the care of her
own sex. We haven't power at all. The legislative bodies
of this nation have been almost snowed under with our petitions and all to no purpose; but we must keep on trying, and
band ourselves together and demand the right; we must preach
and pray and exhort, and never cease; that is all we can do.
Those of you who have read Victor Hugo's beautiful book,
Ninety-three, know that the interest centers on three little
children who had been carried away as hostages and placed
in an upper room in the great tower of La Tourgee, and their
mother has wandered for days and weeks over the fields and
through the valleys and on the highways, in search of them.
She has besought everyone she has met to aid her to find
her children; finally at last, weary, dispirited, almost over-
borne, her feet bleeding as they had been torn by the briars
and thorns along the way she had come--at last she reaches
a ravine, and yonder on the other side is the tower of La
Tourgee, just being besieged by the peasant army; they have
set fire to the tower, and, as the mother peers over, almost
frantic, she catches a glimpse of her children, looking out of
an upper window, far beyond her reach, and there, helpless
and despairing, she sends up one great, terrible, heart-
rending cry, a cry in which all maternity seems to be cen-
tered--a cry so terrible that it pierces the heart of all who
hear. Those hard-handed peasants pause in their work of
destruction; those soldiers stop their bloody carnage; and one
hard man, a representative of the aristocracy, cold-blooded
and violent, hating the peasantry, that man's heart is touched
by this cry of motherhood, and he turns back, takes the key
from his pocket, unlocks the iron door, climbs up--up--
through the flames to the upper room, and passes down the
children one by one into the hands of their mother, amid the
shouts of the soldiers of both parties.

Now, we are like that peasant woman. We see our
children hedged about with difficulties, surrounded by temptation, shut in with the evils of the world. We see our sons
demoralized, our daughters outraged, our hands are tied;
there is nothing that we can do but to cry, to cry aloud and
spare not until our voices shall reach from ocean to ocean;
until the very heavens shall rend asunder, until some man
shall be found, strong enough and good enough, pierced by
our cry, to unlock the door of legislation, and give to the
motherhood of America an opportunity to protect her children.

My colleagues in the committee of resolutions told me

that we must not antagonize, that we must say something sweet,
pleasant, and respectful.   Friends, this is not a time for
pleasant things to be said.   If we had freedom, complacency
and compliments would be in order; but, when women are
outraged, when they are shut up in dens of infamy, ofttimes
beguiled there, when they are beaten, bruised and killed, and
nobody cares for them and the womanhood of this nation are
in bonds, it is not a time for pleasant words; it is a time to
call out for assistance, and we shall not call in vain.   There
is a God of justice over all, and he will overturn and overturn, and overturn, until the right triumphs.

> Still to earnest souls, the sun
> Rests on towered Gideon,
> And the moon of Ajalon
> Lights the battle grounds of life.
> To our aid the strong resources,
> Hidden powers and giant forces,
> And the high stars in their courses
> Mingle in our strife.

We shall conquer.   Some of you remember during the
conflict between Protestant and Catholic in the old time of the
Protestant Reformation, that some one, in describing the situation said: "The Protestants had no power at all, for the
Pope had with him the King of Spain, the King of Sardinia,
the King of France, and the Emperor of Germany; but as
for these poor devils, the Protestants, they had nobody but
God Almighty on their side."   We have against us the Congress of the United States, and the legislatures of the several
States, and the courts, and the newspapers, and the minister,
but we have God Almighty on our side and we shall conquer.

Address Delivered Before the Government
Congress of the World's Exposition,
Chicago

The government of the United States is the product of all the experiments in government which men have made in all the generations of the past.

The nations have travailed together in pain, until now, that a republic, might be born.

Christianity has expressed itself in a government which, theoretically at least, exists for the good of the people and is obedient to their will.

Inspiration reached its high water mark in the principles of the Declaration of Independence, that "All are born free and equal entitled alike to life, liberty and the pursuit of happiness," and the effort to realize this in law and institutions constitutes the glory of the first century of our national life.

It would be too much to expect, that, at one bound, a government should reach the perfect ideal of the Democracy of Christianity, in which the humblest human being should be recognized as standing on a spiritual plane, above all the wealth, honors, princes and kings, powers and potentates of the world, and commanding the resources of the earth for his good. Through many misunderstandings and much tribulation, through many trials of partial and unjust measures and incomplete fulfillment of the promise made to the world, we have slowly emerged from allegiance to class distinctions, prejudices of race and color, clamors for state sovereignty and have now placed ourselves on the roll of the Great Nations of the earth. And although, as the name implies, composed of united states, still the unity and the individuality of our nation is settled for all time. Our government

preserves its national unity in dealing with foreign powers,
it declares war and makes treaties of peace, it protects its
own rights and interests, on sea and land. Its single executive officer ranks with the great monarchs of the old world,
and wherever our flag unrolls its stars and stripes the rights
and dignity of American citizens are respected. We are one
nation. It was the people of the United States who ordained
and established the constitution to preserve the blessings of
liberty for themselves and their posterity. Says a prominent
author, in writing on this subject, "Surely words of such em-
phatic meaning were not chosen by accident or without design.
They tell us that the constitution is a supreme, fixed and
abiding law; ordained and established so that it might make
of the people from whose will it was born one permanent,
powerful and abiding nation."

There is then a United States government and a United
States citizenship. Our constitution distinctly states who are
to be citizens of the United States, viz; those persons "born
or naturalized in the United States." The naturalization laws
of this country provide for a five-year probation during which
the foreign born man may familiarize himself with the principles of our government and the duties of citizenship in a
great free republic; and place himself en rapport with the
spirit and purpose of our people, and, thus prepared, he
takes an oath to support the constitution, he abjures allegiance to all foreign powers, and receives the crown of sovereignty which belongs to the citizen of the United States.

Evidently it was the purpose of the framers of this
government that the citizens of the republic should govern
the country, that representatives in Congress should hold
places at the will of the people of this nation and should represent the interests of its citizens. How far we come short
of realizing this ideal will be seen by the different states.
We find that instead of a government of the people of the
United States, the power is vested, very largely, in men
who are not citizens, who have contributed neither to our
material, intellectual or spiritual enrichment, in time of
peace, nor defended the nation in time of war; men who do
not speak our language, whose names are neither on the tax
roll nor the census list, and whose only claim to rule is
based on a residence of six months or one year in some
frontier district. At the same time more than half of the
citizens, those who by their intelligence and loyalty have
helped to make the country what it is, who pay large taxes
for its support and who are counted in the basis of repre-

sentation, are denied all voice in the government, and compelled to submit to the domination of unnaturalized, alien and often ignorant men.

Among the states, we find the most varied qualifications for suffrage. We have voters who are not citizens and more than half of the adult citizens are not voters. Some of the states practically disfranchise large classes of native born men, most of them disfranchise all women, several of them enfranchise aliens, and when a state which actually recognized the right of the whole people to self government, at last presented itself asking admission to the Union it was only admitted by a small majority, after long and bitter discussion. Surely our Congressmen do not know a republic when they see one.

Like the five franc pieces, issued in the time of the First Napoleon, which bore on one side the legend Republique Française, on the other side Napoleon Empereur, our government holds up to the world the statement that we are a government of the people, and in the same breath proclaims our allegiance to sex aristocracy.

The effect of this is to give the balance of power to irresponsible, ignorant and vicious voters, thus neutralizing the vote of the actual citizens who have made and defended the country and who have great interest at stake in its welfare. How unjust is this to foreign born citizens? We have invited them to come here and find a home, we have said to them that after a proper probation during which they should gain an interest in the country and a knowledge of its needs, they should be placed on an equality with the native born man and endowed with the right to liberty and self-government. But after complying with our conditions and serving out the required five years' term and being duly admitted to the dignities of citizenship they find themselves outvoted and governed by men from foreign nations, who have served no term of probation, who vote for our officers and rule the land, because they have happened to camp four months in Minnesota or six months in Michigan. The census lists do not give us the data from which to determine the relative number of these unnaturalized voters, but the statistics of immigration indicate that in a number of states they held the balance of power, if they are not the actual majority.

When we know that in one day enough Poles arrived in a great western city to turn it, at the next election, from

German to Polish we realize what great wrong is done to
those men who years ago have left homes in the old world
to come here and cultivate the soil and build the cities and
fight the battles and create the wealth of this great nation,
and who by loyal, patient service have earned their right to
citizenship. But if this is a wrong to our <u>naturalized</u> citizens how much greater is the injustice to the <u>native born</u>
men whose fathers founded the nation, in blood and tears, who
have contributed by their character and their money to the
well-being of the commonwealth, who have been educated in
our schools and have spent twenty-one years in preparation
to become intelligent citizens. These men see the land for
which their fathers fought, the sacred institutions which have
cost so many years of toil and sacrifice, the homes they
cherish, the families they love, all given into the hands of
men who do not even speak our language, who are ignorant
of our history, who know nothing of our traditions and are
devoid of that spirit of patriotism which characterizes the
citizens of a great country.

But the crowning outrage and indignity is seen in the
insult offered to American womanhood when the intelligent
loyal mothers of the republic are made politically subject to
tramps, drunkards, idlers, adventurers from all the nations
of the world who have but yesterday landed upon our shores.
No great interest of humanity is safe under these conditions.
The ballot itself is insecure, no man's liberties are safe
when this great fundamental right is left to the caprice of
state legislators or the passing manias which from time to
time sweep over the populace.

It is generally supposed and assumed that the right
of <u>men</u> to vote is secured by the XIVth amendment to the
constitution, which provided for lessening the representation
in Congress whenever the right of suffrage is denied to males.
But it was found at the time the XIVth amendment was passed
that it was insufficient to protect the colored man in the right
of suffrage, white men preferred power in their own states,
to a larger representation in Congress; it will always be insufficient to protect men when for any cause there is a greater desire in the majority for local supremacy than for representation in Congress.

The farther we get from the time of the passage of
the XIVth and XV amendments, the more we all see how unworthy they are of the crisis which brought them forth and
of the great document of which they made a part; they are a

makeshift, serving a temporary political purpose, and designed for the protection of a single class. It is unworthy
of the fundamental law of a great and composite people, that
it should recognize special classes.

The Constitution of the United States should be a charter of liberties for all citizens through all time. What a de-
scent from the swelling preamble in which the people in order "to establish justice, insure domestic tranquility, and to
secure the blessings of liberty to themselves and their posterity," are said to ordain and establish this constitution, to
the fifteenth amendment in which, after seventy-five years
experience of slavery, the right of suffrage is secured only
to two or three millions of black men, and all other men,
and all women black or white, are left to be the sport of
demagogues and political tricksters, dependent for liberty
upon the chance favor of aliens and those whom they have
elected.

No man's liberties are safe when the right of suffrage
upon which all other rights depend, is to be limited or extended according to the whims of legislators, the caprice of
party politicians, or the passing craze of majorities.

The Constitution of the United States should not only
declare who are citizens, but it should guarantee to every
citizen, black or white, native or foreign born, rich or poor,
man or woman the right to cast one free ballot at every public election and to have that ballot honestly counted. It is
not an impossible supposition that the time may come when
in spite of the provision for lessening representation when
males are disfranchised, large classes of American men will
lose their right to vote. The free ballot and the fair count
will be demanded in vain, north as well as south.

In the conflict of nationalities and religions so immi-
nent in our country, what more likely than that in some state
or states whole classes of men will be disfranchised upon
some pretext which shall suit the will or serve the purpose
of the reigning majority. We have but to recall the bitter-
ness of the Know Nothing conflict of a generation ago and to
note the ready response to the cry of "America for Americans" today to see upon what uncertain tenure our foreign
population hold their liberties; and on the other hand the
great numbers of foreign people in some of the new states,
together with their manifest determination to establish here
the customs, traditions, laws and languages of the old world,

make us tremble for the rights of the native born.   Already
in some states ... English is no longer recognized as the
national and state language, the native born people are taxed
to print, at public expense, public documents in various European languages; already the great Lords and Barons of Europe hold extensive tracts of land in our country, and we
know not how soon the desire of political power, pecuniary
gain or religious supremacy may lead them to wish to control the elections of a state.   Whenever such a time comes,
our present voting system gives to foreign potentates the
power to do their will with us.   We are entirely at their
mercy.

The fifteenth amendment providing that no man shall
be disfranchised on account of race, color or previous condition of servitude does indeed protect the Negro man, but
no one else, unless we accept Benjamin Butler's witty sug-
gestion that widows are disfranchised on account of a previous condition of servitude, and in the absence of all reason
for woman's disfranchisement, except for subjection in the
past, we might well claim that ages of servitude were previous enough to open this door to liberty for all women citizens.

By our present voting system our House of Representatives becomes an incongruous gathering, its members represent different constituencies in the states from which they
come.   The representative from Ohio or Iowa has been elected
by and represents the male citizens of twenty-one years of
age in those states while the Congressman from Minnesota,
Wisconsin, or Michigan, represents a great class of male
voters who are not citizens but by a brief residence have obtained the right to govern the nation.   In those states where
there is a large alien population, it is possible that policy or
necessity might justify the voting of unnaturalized men, in
local elections; but surely none can claim that they should be
allowed to help make laws for adjoining states where no such
alien population exists and where a different policy obtains.
That clause in our constitution which provides that the qualifications for electors to the House of Representatives shall be
the same as for the most numerous branch of the state legislature has become injurious in its effects, it opens the door
to gross injustice, and puts in peril the liberties of the loyal
citizens of the republic.

Great changes have been made in the character and
condition of our people since that clause was adopted, and
these "new occasions teach new duties."

The time has come when we should demand that there should be uniformity in the election of the members of our great national legislative body; here at least the will of the actual citizens of the United States should be made effective.

Let the alien population govern their several communities, if they must, but let our great national legislature be composed of men or women who represent the citizens of the United States in the several states from which they come.

The evils above indicated are quite generally recognized and have led to the popular cry that we must stop immigration.

But we cannot afford to cut ourselves off from all these sources of power, we have no right to shut out the waiting people and we cannot do it if we would. "The earth is the Lord's and the fullness thereof, the world and they that dwell therein." These mountains and valleys, these fertile prairies and flowing rivers, these mines of gold and silver and lead and iron and coal, these quarries of marble and granite, these broad lakes with their ever-changing hues and forms of beauty were not made by man's hand, they were not created by the Constitution of the United States or they do not belong to its citizens; they were given by God to his children; and it is because our fathers recognized this fatherhood of God and brotherhood of man and welcomed to our fair land the people from all the countries of the world that our nation has grown to its present magnificent proportions with its glorious record and its inspiring promise of the future.

Every nation has contributed of its kind to help us in subduing nature, thus increasing our wealth and making the earth yield of her abundance for the service of man. The Irishman has drained our marshes and tunneled our mountains and built our railroads. The patient German has cultivated our fields and made the desert blossom as the rose. The ingenuity of the Scandinavian has set in motion the wheels of machinery in our great cities giving remunerative industry to multitudes. The songs of the Celtic bards have swept over the land filling it with music, while the facile Frenchman has brought his nice discrimination and his love of the beautiful to perfect our civilization; and the end is not yet. The undeveloped resources of this country are beyond our ability to imagine, but we know that it is immense, and we need but well directed labor to realize the wildest dream of the enthusiast.

The gigantic wall of the Rocky Mountains rears its
head to heaven filled with uncounted treasure; the vast prairies of the West are still uncultivated, invention is daily cre-
ating new forms of industry and our great need is of honest,
faithful, skillful laborers.   Every people can bring some talent, skill, strength, ingenuity to help in gaining our dominion
over this western continent, not to one man or one nation is
it given the work to do but everyone must bring of his kind
and contribute his part toward building here a great national
temple to the Lord.   Let them come from the overcrowded
cities of Europe, from the legendary lands of the Orient,
from the mysterious regions of interior Africa, from the
distant islands of the ocean.   America is not for Americans,
it is for humanity.   Only let them come honestly, with a purpose of conforming themselves to our civilization, adopting
our republican ideas, submitting to our laws and serving out
a fitting term of preparation to become United States citizens.
It is no remedy for existing evils to say we should deny the
ballot to the foreign born.   We could not govern this immense
number and variety of people by force, the ballot is at once
the instrument of their education and the guarantee of their
good behavior; we do not wish to disfranchise them; it is the
glory of our government that it offers equal rights and privileges to all nationalities and protects them all alike.   Only
by throwing upon them the responsibility of self government
shall we be able at last to blend all in one great free nation,
which shall combine the virtues of all the nations.   And it is
right, reasonable and practicable to require of all that they
should become acquainted with the country and familiar with
its institutions before they undertake to govern it.   We have
a right to demand that before they undertake to govern the
country or to determine its policy by their vote, they should
gain the interest, responsibility and patriotic enthusiasm which
characterizes the loyal citizen.

We owe it to our native born people and to our naturalized brothers to give to them the sovereignty of this nation.   We owe it to civilization, to humanity and to God to
protect this republic, founded in prayer, baptized in the blood
of heroes, and dedicated to liberty; from being destroyed by
ignorance and vice.

The statistics of immigration will show that at least
a million and a half of men of voting age have come into this
country within the last five years, the greater part of them
are scattered about in those nineteen states that allow unnaturalized men to vote.   They are enough to carry the elections

in those states and to determine the fate of the nation. By
limiting the franchise to actual citizens we shall cut off a
million ignorant, irresponsible, reckless voters and by al-
lowing all citizens to vote we shall bring in as voters, the
mothers of the republic, the school teachers, writers, think-
ers, preachers, patriots, students of political economy, those
who have most at stake in the government, for they are the
appointed guardians of the home. The right to vote should be
the distinguishing characteristic of the United States citizen.
Aristotle defines a citizen as "one who participates in the
legislative and judicial authority of the state" and, until the
decision of our Supreme Court in the case of Mrs. Minor,
citizenship, in a republic, was understood to imply a right
to vote.

The United States of America is the first country in
the world to allow itself to be governed by aliens.

It is a policy as unwise and unsafe as it is unheard
of and unjust.

It is necessary for self-preservation that we should
immediately so amend our constitution as to make the ballot
the insignia of citizenship, thus securing the right of suffrage
to all citizens as long as the constitution shall stand, and
making that document the sheet anchor of American liberty.
This would add to our national dignity by securing to American citizens the most valuable of all rights. Citizenship
would be crowned with honor for it would mean the right to
life, liberty and the pursuit of happiness, and the power to
protect these at the ballot box. Grander than the boast of
the Roman citizen--"I was free-born," would be the proud
endowment of the man who could say, "I am a citizen of the
United States, and as such I rise above all superficial and
accidental distinctions of birth, condition, nationality or sex.
I am a child of God endowed with all the liberty of the human being." Such an amendment would make our constitution
no longer the instrument of a faction, affording an imaginary
protection to a limited class of men and providing for a male
oligarchy, but a charter of human rights, placing in the hands
of every American citizen that symbol of liberty, the ballot.
The Constitution of the United States should recognize no
classes, nationalities or conditions; it should know only United
States citizens and make them all free. Such an amendment
would save our government from its present perils, first, because it would raise the standard of sincerity and truth; we
should be, what we now only pretend to be, a republic. This

alone would infuse a spirit of truth and justice into our councils and impart moral stamina to our public men. Next, because introducing a great body of women voters, the majority of whom are native born, intelligent and responsible, would strengthen good men and give added power to the forces which array themselves on the side of order, purity and righteousness.

There is virtue enough in the country to save the country, but at present a large part of the virtue is unrecognized. There is good enough in the country to outvote the evil ten times over if there were only a free ballot and a fair count. There is Americanism enough here to maintain and develop our free institutions in the interest of the highest humanity, but it is denied a voice in the government. Let us have a fair field, a free ballot secured by the Constitution of the United States and the evils that now beset us would vanish like the winter's snow before an April sun. Our government would take new lease of life and our nation stand before the world for ages as the guardian of the rights of man.

Such an amendment would be received by the people with unbounded joy. Everywhere there is complaint of the impurity of our politics and of the injustice of our present suffrage laws. Should the next congress place such an amendment before the Legislatures of the several states, it would be adopted within two years, and we should rejoice in a renovated and saved nation. Will it have the courage to do this?

An Address Delivered Before the Parliament
of Religions at the Hall of Columbus,
Art Institute, Chicago

It is a significant and encouraging sign, that in this great
parliament of religions so much time is given to practical
questions, such as are suggested by intemperance, crime,
the subordination of woman and other subjects of a similar
character. The practical applications of religion are today
of more importance than philosophical speculation. All the
religions of the world are here, not to wrangle over theological differences or forms or modes of worship, but to
join hands in one grand heroic effort for the uplifting of Humanity. Coming from the most remote regions of the earth,
from distant India, China, and the Islands of the Ocean the
representatives to this Parliament, together, bow before that
God who is

Father of all in every age,
In every clime adored,
By Saint, by Savage and by Sage,
Jehovah, Jove or Lord.

All the sects in Christendom, forgetting their differences and rejoicing that we are all one common brotherhood,
unite today in a general warfare against the world, the flesh
and the Devil. We live in a humanitarian age when religion-
ists and theologians are asking not so much how best to secure an interest in the real estate of the Eternal City as how
they may make this earth habitable for God's children. Not
how they may appease the wrath of an offended deity and pur-
chase their own personal salvation hereafter, but how they
can bless their fellow men, here and now. "If ye love not
your brother whom ye have seen how can ye love God whom
ye have not seen?" Theology as represented by all the more
intelligent sects today presents the goodness of God as revealed in the spirit of love which lights up a Universe with
joy and seeks to bless man, the child of God.

131

True genius, in such an age, should occupy itself, not with artificial creations which have no bearing upon daily life but should rather seek to open doors of opportunity, to relieve want and distress and to overcome evil. The real poetry is not found in tropes and figures, does not waste itself in words, however beautiful, but expresses itself in that noble action which is inspired by the life which comes from God.

The highest art is that which unites the useful with the beautiful and glorifies the common round of daily toil. The best religion is that which does most to serve mankind and the true church is that which most reveals the universal love of God looking forward with hope and faith to the fulfillment of the promise of the "One Fold and one Shepherd." But poetry, art and religion are confronted in their progress with the real and terrible evils which mar the beauty and glory of the world. "Man's inhumanity to man makes countless thousands mourn." The awful fact of crime is before us every day.

The cause and cure of Crime is one of the most important questions that can engage the attention of theologian, philanthropist or statesman. In the complex society of modern times, crimes are multiplied, appearing in new forms and disguised and concealed by the methods which our larger knowledge and many inventions make possible. In our country, where are gathered a great variety of people representing all nations, customs and languages, society is necessarily heterogeneous and in the conflict of interests, the greed of gain is awakened, and angry passions are aroused. In the mad rush for the wealth of the world, every man is striving to be foremost; rivalry and selfishness prompt to crime; opportunities for escape are many, and consequently violations of law are frequent and therefore there is pressing need that we should consider what can be done to remedy these evils, lessen crime and out of these varied elements to present at last the perfected, well-rounded human character which shall combine all the best qualities of the various nations and people congregated here, while at the same time eliminating the vices and weakness of each one.

The causes usually given for crime are many such as poverty, evil associations, intemperance, etc. But these are rather the occasions than the causes of criminal conduct. The true philosopher looks behind all these and finds in inherited tendencies one of the most fruitful causes of crime. "The fathers, and the mothers too, have eaten sour grapes and the children's teeth are on edge." It is not the intoxicating cup, but the weak will which causes drunkenness; not the gold within easy reach, but the avaricious mind which prompts to robbery; it is not the weakness of the victim, but the angry passions of the murderer which makes the blood flow. A careful study of the subject by means of statistics has shown that evil deeds, in a very large proportion of cases, can be traced back to the evil passions cherished by the immediate ancestors of the wrongdoer and our means of tracing such connections are so limited that we really know but a small part of the whole truth. A few years ago public attention was called to a widely circulated pamphlet which gave a history of the Jukes family which for generations had been characterized by acts of lawlessness and crime, the taint seemed to extend to every ramification of the family, the awful record showing that out of many hundreds only one or two had escaped idiocy or criminality.

The story of Margaret the mother of criminals is familiar to all. Margaret was a poor, neglected, ignorant inmate of the alms house in one of the counties of New York State, her progeny were found in the poor houses and jails of that region for generations.

In a recent report of one of our great reformatories, the superintendent says: "The investigations and experience of the past year have served to strengthen the opinion that physical degeneracy is a common cause of criminal conduct" which statement confirms the theory that in the majority of cases the criminal is a man badly born. So true is it that in all the relations of life men are dependent upon other men and each one is interested to have everybody else do right, especially his own ancestors. Dipsomania is now almost universally recognized as an inheritance from the drinking habits of the past and all the evil passions of men bear fruitage in after generations in various forms of crime. Recently a man escaped from one of our state prisons by killing two of his guards; he had been charged with matricide and was convicted of murder committed in the most cruel and brutal manner and without any apparent motive. The crime attracted much attention from the fact that he had been reared with great care and tenderness by wise and good parents. At the time of his trial it was shown that the woman he had killed was not, as he had supposed, his own mother but that his reputed parents had adopted him, as an infant in a distant part of the country and had reared and educated him as

their own child.   Little was learned concerning his parentage
except that his father was a murderer.   Thus in spite of education and circumstances the inherent tendency to murder as-
serted itself and the crime of the father was repeated again
in the son.

This is but one instance, but it is the type of many
that are familiar to students of this subject, all showing that
the criminal is often the victim of the mistakes, the evil passions, the crimes of those who went before.   As the drinking
habit results, in after generations, in epilepsy, insanity and
various forms of nervous disease, so other evil passions re-
appear in different guises and give birth to a great variety
of crimes.   Not only is the criminal the victim of the blunders of the past but he, in turn becomes the author of a
chain of consequences, which entail poverty and crime and
irresponsibility upon the generations that come after him.

What can we do to check this great tide of criminality
which perpetuates itself thus from generation to generation,
gathering ever new strength and force with time?   How stop
this supply of criminals?

There is but one answer, men must be better born,
our remedial measures are feeble and ineffectual unless we
can begin at the fountain head; for while we are reforming
one criminal one hundred more are born.   We must have
better mothers.   We are learning that not only the sins of
the father, but the mistakes and unfortunate conditions of the
mothers, bear terrible fruitage, even to the third and fourth
generation.   God has entrusted the mother with the awful responsibility of giving the first direction to human character.

In the long months which precede the birth of the young
spirit, what communion of angels may elevate and inspire her
soul thus giving the promise of the advent of a heavenly mes-
senger who should proclaim peace on earth good will to men!
Or what demons of pride, revenge, avarice, [jealousy], may
preside over the development of the new life sending forth,
upon earth an avenger, to lift his hand against every man,
to blast the joys of life and to weigh like an incubus upon
society!   Woman becomes thus an architect of human life
with all its possibilities of joy or sorrow, of virtue or vice
of victory or defeat, and it was because of this momentous
mission that she was, not only given joint dominion with man
over the earth, but was made to be supreme in the home and
in the marriage relation.

Old and New Testament Scriptures alike, announce the
Divine fiat that man is to leave all things, his father and his
mother if need be, and cleave unto his wife. His personal
preferences, his ambitions, his business of the world, his
early affections, all must be subordinate to this one great
object of the marriage relation, the formation of noble human characters; and in this creative realm [woman] is to
rule supreme, she must be the arbiter of the home, that in
her Divine work of moulding character she may surround herself with such conditions and win to herself such heavenly
communions that her children shall be indeed heirs of God
bearing upon their foreheads the stamp of the Divine. But
how far have we come short of this grand ideal, how dis-
obedient are we to the scriptural requirement, when the customs of society and the laws of the land demand that a woman, in marriage, shall give up home, business, ambition--
everything, even her name to be lost in oblivion, and her individuality merged in that of another!

When in some of our marriage ceremonies she is required to promise implicit obedience to her lord and master
and in so called Christian states she is bound by law to work
all her lifetime for board and clothes, it is evident that we
are not fulfilling the Scriptural law. No wonder the world is
cursed with cowards, idiots and criminals when the mothers
of the race are in bondage. Only in an atmosphere of freedom can woman accomplish her grand destiny. Napoleon, on
being asked what France most needed, replied, good mothers.
But I say, what France, America and all lands need is a
free motherhood. The woman who in ignorance or delusion
has been led to marry a man tainted with epilepsy, insanity
or drunkenness must not be compelled to send forth to the
world poor, defective, dwarfed caricatures of humanity, whose
poor round of life will be bounded by the walls of a prison
or the wards of a hospital. Helen Gardner well says, "Moral
idiots, like Jessie Pomperoy and Reginald Berchall in life,
Pecksniffs, Becky Sharps and Fred Harmons in fiction will
continue to cumber the earth as long as conditions continue
to breed them." The race is stamped by its mothers, the
fountain will not rise higher than its source, men will be no
better than the mothers that bear them and as woman is elevated, her mental vision enlarged and her true dignity established, will her sons go forth armed with a native power to
uphold the right, trample out iniquity and overcome the world.

The battle for womanhood is the battle for the race,
upon her dignity of character and position depends the future

of humanity. We shall have taken the first and all important
step in doing away with crime and lessening the number of
criminals when we have emancipated motherhood. Women
who are politically subordinate and financially dependent,
pauperized in the home and unrecognized in the state can
not bequeath to their sons high moral courage, independence of spirit or that uprightness which makes a man seek
to accomplish noble aims by straightforward methods. The
degradation of women is the greatest crime of the world and
it is the foundation of all other crimes. The emancipation
of women means society redeemed and humanity saved. With
the elevation of women, education will become more effective.
Not only will children be better born but there will be higher
ideals, new incentives and the whole scope of education and
reform will be enlarged.

Men are more learned than women, they have behind
them centuries of education and culture; at their command
are all the great universities and libraries of the world;
theirs is the higher education of experience in the actual
business of life, but more powerful than experience, education, libraries or universities is a mother's love.

The Universalist church which I have the honor to
represent stands for the humanitarian element in religion.
It recognizes the fatherhood of God and the brotherhood of
man. We believe in a God who has made all things good
and beautiful in their time and whose supreme and benefi-
cent law will work out the final victory of the good. We believe that even the poorest, most ill-born, most misdirected
human being possesses capabilities of goodness which are in
their nature divine and indestructible, and which must at last
enable him, by God's grace, to rise above weakness and folly
and sin, and to share in it the inheritance of eternal life.
We believe that love is the potent influence which shall at
last win all souls to holiness and to God, love, exemplified
and made effective through the life, the labors, the teachings,
the death and resurrection of Jesus Christ, who came to be
a propitiation for the sins of the whole world.

And, so believing, our church stands for those humane
methods of dealing with the criminal, which, while protecting
society, shall at the same time seek the reformation of the
erring one.

Regarding human life as too sacred a gift to be placed
in the hands of human courts, we oppose capital punishment

and we make unceasing war upon such kinds of prison discipline as tend to harden and brutalize the criminal. We ask
that penal legislation shall consider the salvation of the guilty
and that prisons shall be made reformatories where a wise,
well-directed and sympathetic Christian charity shall devise
methods to reform the criminal and return him to society a
redeemed man and a useful citizen.

But while so few people believe in the possible salvation of the erring, while the spirit of true Christian love is
still so rare and its intelligent application to the practical
work of the world so little sought, how can officers be found
to fitly manage such institutions and conduct them in the interest of the highest humanity? While our legislatures are
still so much imbued by the material and utilitarian spirit of
previous ages of selfishness, how secure [are] such laws as
shall represent the philanthropy and the sympathy of a truly
Christian people?

It can scarcely be expected that the politician who
shouted the war cry of his party the loudest in the last campaign will have the nice discrimination, the ready sympathy
and Christian charity necessary to minister to the diseased
soul; yet he is the man that our system of political prefer-
ment would place at the head of any state reformatory institution. Great men, learned theologians we have, but how
rarely do they combine with their learning charity for the
erring and that attention to minor details and significant
symptoms which is so necessary in reforming men. The
Spanish have a proverb that "An ounce of mother is better
than a pound of clergy" and it is true that a mother's tenderness will do more to touch the hard heart of the criminal
than the most able presentation of the most powerful preacher.

We need, in dealing with these humanitarian questions,
the mother's sympathy with her little ones. Mothers, who
alone know at what great cost a human life has been given
to the world, should help to make the laws which affect the
condition and decide the earthly destiny of their children.

Our legislators have been so much occupied with questions of tariff and taxes, of silver and coinage and other pecuniary interests that they have, in a measure, neglected the
higher objects of legislation, namely the development of a
redeemed and perfected humanity. When the mothers sit in
council those subjects which affect the improvement of society, the protection of the weak, the reformation of the wicked,

the education of the youth, the elimination of the unfortunate
and dangerous classes, will be made prominent. Less money
will be expended in great public demonstrations and more in
educational enterprises, less show in inaugural balls and pro-
cessions and more of the wealth and talent of the nation will
be given to reclaiming the fallen.

As in the sick room it is the mother's tender touch
that soothes the child's pain and calls back the glow of health,
so in this sin-sick world, it must be the loving sympathy of
mothers that shall win back the erring and restore them to
mental health and moral beauty. It is the glory of Christianity that it has recognized and enthroned womanhood.

The great master first revealed himself as the Messiah
to a woman. He wrought his first miracle at the command of
a woman, and as a recognition of the supremacy of motherhood; he revealed the great truths that he came to bring to
women, and he sent women forth to proclaim the risen Lord,
and so today he commands women to go abroad publishing the
Gospel of a world's salvation, not only by words but by life
and by deeds. And shall men, churches or governments dare
longer to prohibit women from obeying the command and fulfilling the Divine decree? All reforms wait for woman's
freedom. It is promised that the seed of the woman shall
bruise the serpent's head. But it must be the seed of a
woman who is intelligent, independent and free. The only
effectual remedy for crime is the emancipation of motherhood.

WHY THE CHURCH SHOULD DEMAND
THE BALLOT FOR WOMEN
(n. d.)

The ballot is the instrument by which men express their opinions on public questions; it is the voice of the people concerning the general good.

The Church is the organized body of the best people, that is, people pledged to righteousness.

Should not the best people speak on questions of public interest!

The Church is composed in considerable part of women.

Should not this large body of church members express an opinion on questions pertaining to the common good!

The Church is the repository of Christian truth; it stands for honesty and purity and it aims at the highest things; should not its whole influence be felt at the ballot box?

The question has been asked, why does not the Church exert more influence in favor of justice and honesty and purity in our Commonwealth? At this time when the people are appalled by the revelations of graft and dishonesty and immorality which are being made, when the rottenness of our business and social life is being exposed, when machine politics and corrupt politicians by their unwarranted methods are threatening the very life of our republican institutions, why is not the Church heard from? Why does it not effectively and with power withstand the evil influences that are sapping the foundations of our Christian civilization? It would seem that the Church could do this and ought to do it. The great majority of the people in this country are church attendants, many of them members. Every Sunday and often on weekday evenings they listen to presentations of the moral and spiritual and practical questions of the time. Able, cultured and consecrated men or women are employed to set forth the

truths concerning Christian duty and Christian life and their
application to the problems of the various communities to
which they belong; these things are enforced by argument
and oratory; seasons of prayer are appointed for the success of purity, temperance, honesty; for the prosperity of
the country and the permanency of our government; the streets
and the byways are searched to bring in the people and enlist
them in good things. A great number of women spend all
their spare time in the work of the Church, bringing to it
their grand enthusiasm and earnest consecration; no other
organization commands such general allegiance, enlists such
numbers and secures such active interest as the Church. Under these circumstances it would seem that the Church would
really be the governing body in the Commonwealth, that it
would be the power behind the throne influencing all the various organizations and by its vote really deciding elections,
practically determining the character of the officers chosen,
and thus dominating the course of legislation. All this the
Church might do, that it does not do it is painfully manifest.

Why does it not do it? Our public officials do not
consult the clergymen about the best method of securing order or maintaining moral principles in the town.

No politician in making up his slate ever asks concerning a proposed candidate for office whether he will be
acceptable to the Church.

The preferences of the brewers, the prejudices of the
stock gamblers, the interests of the corporations are care-
fully considered by these guardians of the public welfare, but
religion is supposed to be something wholly outside of all
questions of general interest and not to be thought of in this
connection. Now why are these things so? Why does not
the Church exert its legitimate influence on public affairs?

A consideration of the situation will show why this
great body of Christian workers is robbed of its power for
good.

The Church lacks the element of power in a republic,
it has no means of making its principles effective in the deciding public questions; it cannot express itself on public affairs; it is practically a disfranchised body.

So large a proportion of its members and so great a
part of the congregations are women that they give character

to the whole body and limit the amount of power which it can exercise. The Church is hampered, crippled, weakened by the disfranchisement of the majority of its members.

Exact statistics are scarcely obtainable as to the relative number of men and women in the churches, but it is safe to suppose that in the Catholic churches there are at least as many women as men. A very prominent and judicious Congregationalist minister writes that that is about the proportion in his denomination and Mrs. Clara C. Chapin, writing a tract for the W. C. T. U., says that "it is authoritatively stated that in the whole country the women constitute two-thirds of the membership of the Protestant churches," but observation of the attendants upon the regular church service in almost any denomination will show a much larger percentage of women, on all of whom the preacher's sermon is lost, so far as influence on public affairs is concerned.

Some clergymen have seen and noted this and have accordingly made a demand for a "man's church," and some churches have sought to secure a certain measure of respectability for themselves by establishing men's leagues within the church.

But a church or any other organization for Christian work without women would be an anomalous affair. Women from the very first have been the very life of the Church. The Master revealed Himself specially to women. The first miracle was wrought at the request of a woman. They were last at the cross and first at the sepulchre, and when he rose from the dead he revealed himself first of all to a woman and bade her go and proclaim the risen Lord.

Christianity broke down the old barriers and admitted women to the public assemblies, recognized their right to speak as they were moved and to bear their testimony in the great congregation, and from that day to this Christianity and the Christian Church have been upheld, inspired, sustained and honored by the work of women and a very large proportion of the membership is composed of women.

It is practically impossible to cast them out. We cannot have a man's church; such a church would not be a Christian church, for Christianity recognizes neither Jew nor Greek, nor bond nor free, nor male nor female. But we can have a Christian church composed of intelligent, right-minded human beings, all of whom are interested in the pub-

lic welfare and every one of whom may cast a vote on the
side of good government, thus making the Church a great
power for righteousness in the administration of our public
affairs.

Society today needs the votes of the church women in
settling the great moral problems of our time. The mainte-
nance of the home, the proper environment for the children,
the protection of the poor, all call for the votes of the church
women; and the Church if it would maintain the dignity and
self-respect that belong to such an organization, if it would
do its grandest work, must secure the ballot for its women.

The voting of women will change the ideals of our
statesmanship, substituting humanitarianism for purely financial considerations, bringing to the front the ideals presented
by the Master.

The great problems which are today before the American people calling for solution are moral problems; the age
of brute force is passing and the era of reason and religion
is dawning. Private disputes are no longer settled by the
duel but by law, and international questions are beginning to
be solved by arbitration rather than an appeal to arms, and
though we still flourish the "big stick" and make a show of
our handsome navy on the great oceans, peace societies flourish and peaceful doctrines pervade our country and the attention of the people is turning to subjects which relate to the
improvement of humanity. We are trying to save souls rather
than to destroy lives.

In the work of salvation and regeneration woman finds
one of her most effective fields of labor. The development
of a higher humanity requires the united efforts of the best
men and the best women.

In the government of our cities, in the control of our
systems of education, in the management of jails and prisons
we need the mother's sympathy and ready perception. We
need to put the Christ spirit of peace and goodwill to men
into our institutions, thus driving out the selfish greed and
grafting, the dishonesty, cruelty and carelessness which are
destroying our civilization and threatening the very life of the
government.

President Eliot of Harvard is quoted as saying, "The
present forms of city government are total failures." The

American people, he says, "have not made one success at governing a city." And this is not strange when we consider that much of the vice of the country is concentrated in the great cities; there the gambling hall and the liquor saloon flourish; there unscrupulous corporations have their headquarters; there the speculators and dishonest promoters find their ready victims, and all these classes, speculators, gamblers, liquor dealers, tramps and drunkards, all the powers of evil, have votes, while the forces that make for righteousness, the home, the school and the church, are disfranchised. There is virtue enough in our cities to outvote and govern all the vice; there is goodness enough in our country to control all the evil. There is truth and honesty enough to override and put down dishonesty and graft, but the truth, the honesty, the virtue, the goodness are disfranchised, to a very large extent.

If we could remove the barriers and give all a fair chance to be heard at the polls we should see how strong and grand and true our American people are. Our cities would be governed in the interest of virtue and honesty and our country would take a new and a higher rank among the nations.

Why should the Church advocate woman's suffrage? Because it cannot do its full work for Christ while more than half of its members have no votes and are mere silent partners.

Second, because when all its members have a voice in public affairs it will become an important factor in our national life. This will command respect and it will multiply members. There will then be no need of a "man's church." The men will all be in church. This will add dignity to our pastors, who now share in the humiliation of woman's disfranchisement, because their constituency is so largely disfranchised. In short, if the Church would secure its own prosperity and its legitimate influence it must ask for all its members a right to cast a vote on all matters of public interest and demand for its women the character and the respect which enfranchisement alone can confer.

The Gordian Knot, which our rulers have placed before us
tied so securely that none have yet been able to untie and no
Alexander has been great enough to cut, is the Woman's Suffrage Knot.

Shall it be untied? Or shall it be cut? And where is
the man who shall appear with the ingenuity to untie or the
courage to cut? The question of Woman's Suffrage is now
so well understood and the necessity for the votes of women
so apparent that it only remains to find a way to accomplish
the desired result. Most men outside the whisky ring, a
few lame politicians and some of the newly enfranchised Indians and Negroes, wish that women had the ballot.

A few years ago the writer had occasion to call on the
lawyers of one of our prominent cities interviewing them on
the subject and was surprised to find them almost to a man
in favor of Woman's Suffrage.

Recently being called upon suddenly for a list of sign-
ers to the Suffrage petition the writer found a ready response;
not more than two in the whole afternoon declining to sign;
and these were not exceptionally radical cities.

The magazines of the day find no subject more popular and no argument better received than one in favor of
Woman's Suffrage. The popular lecturer secures no more
spontaneous applause than when he makes a hit in favor of
the rights of women. These are trifles but they are "straws
that show which way the wind blows." Many more indications
might be brought all pointing to a quite general demand for
the enfranchisement of woman.

Why, then, it might be asked, do women continually
petition in vain? In a country where men rule it would seem
that men could enfranchise women if they so wished.

But the question of how to do it presents itself. The

144

matter is hedged about with difficulties and it calls for a
strong brave man to lead the way; such a man taking a stand
for Woman's Suffrage and pushing it in the various ways
known to political managers would be surprised to find himself so ably supported and so readily carried to victory.

Robert Louis Stevenson explains the enthusiasm which
followed the order of Germanicus to his men "forward; follow the Roman eagles" by saying that in appropriating the
eagles as fellow country men, "Germanicus made allies of
the forces of nature." And brave men in all ages pushing
forward in the line of progress find allies in nature, in the
loyalty of true men, in the grand enthusiasm for humanity
which are ever waiting to respond to an earnest call.

The hero who should bravely and persistently work
for Woman's Suffrage would win his cause and in doing so
make himself immortal. But no great work is done without
effort. The emancipation of woman is the greatest work that
has ever been undertaken in behalf of liberty. The enfranchisement of women of the United States would affect far
more people than were involved in the contest for the emancipation of the slaves; millions more than the number of people of the Colonies in whose behalf our ancestors fought out
the war for Independence; its effect upon society and civilization would be immense. Such work calls for intellectual acumen, courage and persistence. Various methods of accom-
plishing the result have been proposed.

We have been trying these many years to untie the
knot by means of local legislation. Thus far this method
has been largely a failure. The limited suffrage gained here
and there on the subject of schools or other local interests
while good, so far has not had sufficient significance to
awaken general enthusiasm and these laws have in several
cases been declared unconstitutional and are questionable in
all cases.

The action of state legislatures is necessarily slow,
several states requiring a constitutional amendment to be
adopted by two successive legislatures; sometimes requiring
a 2/3 vote and, in several states, the legislature meets but
once in two years, thus making the process a long one to
even bring the subject before the voters. And then it seems
like an insult to American womanhood to ask intelligent, patriotic citizens, property holders and taxpayers to submit the
question of their rights, in the state they have helped to make,
to the caprices of foreigners, Negroes and Indians, illiterate

drunken and poverty stricken men of all shades. If women
have these rights they should hold them by some more secure tenure than this.

The case has seemed so plain and the measure so just
that some have looked to the courts to cut the Gordian Knot
by deciding that women were citizens and PEOPLE and entitled to be so recognized and this may yet be the solution
of the problem.

An enthusiastic young man recently wrote a letter to
the writer of this article recommending that a case should be
brought and a decision secured from the Supreme Court and
he generously [offered] to aid in defraying the expenses of
such suit. But, of course, he did not know of the various
contradictory decisions which the Supreme Court has already
rendered. And it should be remembered that courts are necessarily bound to the past; they look for precedents and are
governed largely by former decisions. A new subject like
this presents points not involved in their line of study and
on which they have not thought. Forward movements have
more to hope from legislation than from court decisions.

For some thirty years or more Mrs. Stanton, Miss
Anthony and their followers have been petitioning the Congress for a sixteenth amendment to the constitution of the
United States prohibiting the states from disfranchising citizens on account of sex and this would seem to be the "Line
of Least resistance."

Since in the Congress we have a picked body of men
supposed to be the ablest in the nation and therefore meas-
urably free from unreasonable prejudice--men with their faces
to the future and animated by the spirit of progress--it would
seem that we might hope for intelligent and wise action there,
the more especially as the constitution itself was "ordained
and established" by the "people," without any exceptions and
the principles behind the constitution recognize the rights of
all. But we are told that amending the constitution is impossible. Statesmen who have interests which they desire to
see expressed in amendments acknowledge their helplessness
and one at least ... of our statesmen has advanced the idea
that the constitution is elastic enough to meet every need and
that, instead of trying to amend that instrument, we should
rather seek new interpretations, enlarge its meanings and
find new and broader applications of its provisions.

It was doubtless in accordance with this thought that

Mr. Wm. Loughbridge and Benjamin F. Butler in 1871 urged
upon the House of Representatives the adoption of the following resolution: Resolved by the House of Representatives,
"That the right of suffrage is one of the inalienable rights
of Citizens of the United States, subject to the regulations
by the states through equal and just laws." This resolution
was defended by the most able and seemingly unanswerable
arguments. In speaking of the courts as a means of establishing the rights of women to vote, Mr. Butler says: "We
respectfully submit that with regard to the competency and
qualifications of electors for members of this House (the
House of Representatives) the courts have no jurisdiction.
This House is the sole judge of the election returns and qualifications of its own members and it is for this House alone
to decide upon a contest who are and who are not competent
and qualified to vote."

The practical objection to the resolution [offered] by
Mr. Butler is his statement that suffrage is an "inalienable
right." Many people today are disposed to maintain that suffrage is not a right but something conferred and it is not
necessary for us to enter into this discussion of whether it
is a right or a privilege. The ballot will be as valuable to
women if conceded because their votes are needed as if given
as a right.

The question for us to ask is whether the constitution
by its wording or by implication makes it possible for women
to vote for any office? What was the intent of the framer?
What does the history of our government show? When the
framers of the constitution drew up that document which was
to stand for ages as the Palladium of the liberties of millions
of people, they undertook a new and great work--nothing like
it had ever been attempted before, they had no chart to guide
them over the untraveled sea of democratic legislation. The
government of the people was a new thing under the sun--the
recognition of human beings as such endowed by God with capabilities and deserving of recognition by virtue of their humanity was unknown in the legislation of the old world.

Radical and daring men launched out in the new realm
and demanded a government which should give the will of the
people authoritative expression. On the other hand, many of
the men in the constitutional convention looked back to England for ideals fashioned upon the governments of the old
world; the king, the lords, the commons, loomed large before their mental vision and their wish was to establish a
lesser England in this new world.

Between two such differing conceptions of the work to be done there must necessarily have been conflict, discussion added to discussion--confidence and courage, inspiration and hope on the one side; and cautious conservatism, doubt and fear on the other--slowly the work progressed.

It was the old conflict between the heralds of the new and the guardians of the old, and the result as ever was a compromise. The Senate, corresponding somewhat to the House of Lords, was to be chosen by the legislatures of the several states; its members represented not the people but the states from which they came and they met the demand of the aristocratic portion of the convention.

The President also, was to be chosen by the PEOPLE OF THE STATES in accordance with rules to be made by the state legislatures.

The Judiciary was to be appointed by the President. Thus far the government was aristocratic. There was nothing to correspond to the ideals of the Radicals of a government emanating directly from the people, this was to be secured by placing in their hands the election of the members of the more numerous branch of the National Legislature.

The question of giving the election of members to the people was the very first thing discussed and while it was considered dangerous to trust the people with such power it was finally admitted that an election of the more numerous branch of the National Legislature by the people would introduce a true democratic principle into the government. It was urged that this branch of the legislature ought to know and sympathize with every part of the community and ought, therefore, to be taken not only from the different parts of the republic but also from different districts of the larger members of it. And as that system was to be republican, a direct representation of the people was indispensable. The broadest possible basis it was said ought to be given to the new system.

The national House of Representatives is the organized expression of the democratic spirit of this country; it stands for the democratic idea in our government and the only place in the constitution where the vote of the whole people is called for is that providing for the election of its members.

It is provided: Article I, Section II, Clause I, "The

House of Representatives shall be composed of members
chosen every second year by the PEOPLE of the several
states. "

This is the one saving clause that gives us a right
to claim our government as democratic--here alone "the people" are recognized as choosing representatives.

Even this was not obtained without long controversy.
It was reported in the fourth Randolph resolution but it was
opposed on the ground of the "ignorance of the people." The
discussion on this clause was earnest and long continued arguments on both sides were brought and finally it was adopted.

But the end was not yet. A week after it had been
adopted it was reconsidered on account of what was called
"the unfitness of the people." After much discussion, the
election by the people was carried a second time. Two
weeks later another effort was made to place the election of
the representatives in the hands of the legislatures--again the
advocates of representation by the people stood firm and saved
to us a democratic government in which the people have a
voice in electing the most numerous branch of the National
Congress.

Now, if women are a part of the people they have a
right, under the constitution, to vote for the members of the
House of Representatives. If they are human beings, if they
can think and speak, if they are not wild beasts, or "stocks
or stones or worse than senseless things" they are a part of
the people and if a part of the people entitled to representation. To use the words of our Supreme Court: "The words
people and citizens are synonymous terms. They describe
the political body who, according to our republican institutions, form the sovereignty and who hold the power and conduct the government through their representatives. They are
what we familiarly call 'the sovereign people' and every citizen is one of this people and a constituent member of this
'sovereignty.' "

But we are told that the second clause of the article
in question leaves the whole subject in the hands of the states
by the words "and the electors in each state shall have the
qualifications requisite for the electors in the most numerous
branch of the state legislature." But evidently that clause
was not enacted for the purpose of doing away with the previous clause which gave the election to the people. It is

scarcely probable that having striven to secure a department
of the government to represent the people, the democratic
members have been content with a provision that placed the
election of the members of the House like that of the Senate
and the President in the hands of state legislatures.

The clause evidently relates to such necessary qualifications as age, residence, etc. which are not finally exclusive and which can only be determined locally and hence were
left to the local officers.

It is likely that Randolph and Mason and Wilson and
Madison after for weeks battling for the right of the people
to vote for the members of the House of Representatives
would accept in the same article a clause which made it
possible for states to disfranchise whole classes forever?

To suppose that that clause was intended to permit
the disfranchisement of large proportions of the people is to
make the whole section meaningless and to bring the democratic members of the constitutional convention into contempt,
since they were standing for some department of the government which would be the voice of the people.   Now, if they
inserted a clause which permitted the legislature or the constitution of a state to disfranchise the people, evidently they
must have been caught napping and they were not that kind of
men.   They knew what they were doing and what they wanted
and they were not likely to defeat their own object or to allow it to be defeated by others; and in order to make sure
that in giving to the states the right to formulate conditions
of election they should not give them power to take from the
people their right to vote without recourse, it was provided
in Section IV of the constitution that the Congress may at any
time alter the arrangements made by the states and, as stated
by Mr. Madison, this was done expressly lest some state
should deprive a part of the citizens of the right of suffrage.
Congress is given power in the fourth Section of Article I
"at any time by law to make or alter such regulations, " that
is, the regulations made by the states.   It is also provided
"each house shall be the judge of the election returns and
qualification of its own members. "

Therefore, whenever the House of Representatives
shall be satisfied that in the election of its members the regulations of the states or the qualifications required prevent
the voice of the people from being heard, it is theirs to pass
a law making alterations in these regulations and requiring the

vote of the whole people. President Roosevelt said in his
message of 1904, "The power of the government to protect
the integrity of the elections of its own officials is inherent
and has been recognized and affirmed by repeated declara-
tions of the Supreme Court." And certainly there never was
a more manifest violation of the first clause of Article I than
in the disfranchisement of loyal tax-paying intelligent citizens
by the states; not only is it a glaring injustice to the class
disfranchised and consequent injury to the communities to
which they belong, but it is a violation of the authority of
the National Government in providing for the general welfare.

While in the election of local or state officers there
may be and perhaps ought to be different regulations in regard to the suffrage to suit the varying conditions in the different states, yet, in the election of Federal officers there
should be uniformity.

The character of the constituency determines the quality of the representative and the kind of legislation, and hence
in order to have consistent and harmonious national legislation it is necessary to have uniform suffrage laws for the
election of Federal officers; the election of these officers is
a matter of general interest affecting all the states and determining to some extent their relations to one another.

We have laws governing interstate commerce and making freight rates uniform and many are considering demanding
uniform divorce laws because these subjects relate to the intercourse between the states and are subjects of common interest but how much more is this true of the election of the
National Legislature which is to enact laws, not concerning
local affairs, but touching the whole nation!

We have a uniform method of electing Senators and
Presidents and in order to make our government truly national it is necessary to have a uniformity in electing members of the House of Representatives.

This, then, is the immediate demand with regard to
suffrage and it is in the power of the Congress by law to
require that the votes of women be taken in the election of
its members and that the qualifications for electors for members of the House of Representatives shall be the same
throughout the United States.

This is legislation which affects the internal concerns

of the states GENERALLY as opposed to those which belong
especially to the individual and separate states.   This is not
centralization or the assumption of new powers by the general government but it is the exercise of a power delegated
to the United States by the constitution and necessary to the
protection of the "rights of the people," of which the Congress is the constituted guardian.

Nor is it a reason for inaction that for so many years
the Congress has neglected to pass such law or to assume its
authority in this respect.   Many influences and varied conditions of society have conspired at different times to prevent
such legislation.   But the time is now ripe.   There is a
clearer understanding of the relations of the states to the
general government than ever before; there is a grander conception of the significance of citizenship than in the years
gone by.

Our country, its laws, its institutions and its customs
are more generally appreciated than in the earlier days of
our republic; national pride and public interest are leading
to a more careful survey of our history and a more thorough
study of our constitution.   The people are realizing more than
ever their powers and duties.

One of our great states declares in its constitution "a
recurrence to first principles is absolutely necessary to the
preservation of our liberties."   Such a recurrence to first
principles is what is now required of the House of Representatives.

If amid the complexity of our government and the conflicting interests of opposing parties the necessity of uniformity in the election of Federal officers has been unnoted; if the
comprehensiveness of the word PEOPLE has been forgotten
it is time to recur to first principles and inquire how to secure the vote of the people for their representatives in Congress and to take action looking to uniformity in Federal elections.

It is late to do these things, but it is better late than
never.   For a long time we have been feeling the evil influence of this violation of the constitution and as the years go
by the confusion increases.

One of the most conservative publications of our time
mentions "three evils that are menacing our country today:

1st: Debasement of moral standards in politics
       and business.

2nd: Absorption by a few at unwarranted cost to
       the many of the common wealth

3rd: Unreasonable and violent expression of resent-
       ment by the people.

And all these evils are the result of a lowering of the standards of justice and morality which have followed upon and
been induced by the wrong done to one half of the people in
their disfranchisement.   "He that is guilty in one point is
liable to all."

The restoring of woman's right to vote for members
of the House of Representatives is, it is true, only the one
step but it is a step so important that it would open the door
to larger opportunities; it would be the beginning of the end
of the struggle.   And it is a step which can be taken by the
Congress without an appeal to the state legislatures or a reference to the present voters.   It is easy, practical, constitutional and just.

The Christian Religion teaches the lesson of service, mutual helpfulness. The lesson of the Scriptures is "do as you will be done by" [and] "By love serve one another." It suggests the idea of cooperation, all working together for the common good. "If one member suffer all the members suffer with it." If one member rejoices, all the members rejoice with it. It is upon this idea of mutual helpfulness and cooperation that the Christian civilization is based. Without this thought of cooperation and brotherhood, a Christian civilization would be impossible. When Christianity came it taught a new doctrine. The worth of man. The slave toiling under the master's lash was a man bearing the divine image, therefore worthy of consideration and respect. Then it began to be learned that the human being, child of the great All Father is of more value than all the piled up wealth of the world.

Under this influence tyrannies and despotisms began to give way. Humanity began to rise. Through the centuries this struggle with oppression went on. As Victor Hugo has said: "There has been ever echoing through the halls of time the sound of the wooden shoe ascending and the polished boot descending." Ever the common people, the peasantry, gaining new liberties and new opportunities. Ever the aristocracy, the tyranny or the despotism going down. Little by little man began to realize the rights of the human.

A Christian democracy such as we claim to be here is the outgrowth of this Christian ideal of the worth of man and the duty of all men to work together, cooperating for the common good.

A Christian government is simply a large society in which all unite, first of all for protection, then for improvement, then for the development of the Arts and conveniences of our modern civilization.

Men united together can secure for themselves advan-

tages impossible for the individual. Many of you younger
people belong to some kind of club or society. In this club
you pay your dues, you are bound to contribute your influence and character to the well-being of the club and you expect also complete recognition by the club. You have your
voice in all its proceedings and you expect to do your part
to render the club effective for good.

Now our state is simply a larger club in which we all
unite, paying our dues (that is, our taxes), lending our moral
support to the well-being of the club, and this moral support
is expressed by the ballot. Hence, the ballot becomes the
instrument whereby we make known our wishes with regard
to this great society to which we belong and everyone is under an obligation to do the uttermost for the common good.

The man who neglects to do his part, who fails when
great questions arise to cast his ballot on the right side is
disloyal. He has been well characterized by Mr. Roosevelt
as a coward, a weakling and a Molly coddle.

For many years men have assumed that they alone
were entitled to a voice in this great organization, although
women have contributed in the same way to the common fund
and are prepared to contribute of their intelligence, their
public spirit, their love of virtue to the well-being of the
commonwealth.

It was not the design originally of the framers of our
Government to disfranchise women. The only place in the
Constitution of the United States where the vote is mentioned
is in the provision for the election of members of the House
of Representatives. And there it is stated that all people are
to join in electing its members.

During the long weeks in which the framers of our
constitution labored there was much discussion concerning
this clause. There were those who claimed that it was impossible to allow the people to vote for a public officer.
They claimed that the people were too ignorant and too emotional to be entrusted with the ballot. But such men as Jef-
ferson and Franklin and Hamilton took a different view.
Franklin told them that those who had no voice in electing
the men who made the laws were slaves to those who had a
voice in electing the officers. Three different times this
clause was discussed at length and finally the Democratic
members prevailed and secured this recognition of the whole

people. George Washington is quoted as having said "that by people he understood not merely men, but men and women."

There is no evidence that there was any intention then to discriminate against women. Women were then voting in many states on the same terms with men. It is true very few women voted because there were then property qualifications in most states. The property qualification was one which women could not attain because in a primitive condition of society all women, or nearly all, are married. The proportion of the sexes is about equal or sometimes men outnumbered women. In such a condition of society all women will be married.

According to the old English Common Law the married woman was "merged." Her personality no longer existed. Her property, if she had any, went to the husband, by the act of marriage. If she did any work outside the home her earnings belonged to the husband. In those days at the marriage altar the bridegroom was made to commit perjury. He said "With all my goods I thee endow" when by the act of marriage he purposed to take all her goods and endow her with nothing except the privilege of taking care of him.

Under those conditions, of course, there were very few women who could meet the qualifications of voters. Here and there there might be a wealthy widow and such widows voted.

It was published very extensively during the Taft campaign that his grandmother had been a voter, having been a large property holder she was entitled to vote, and on one occasion when a question of great importance was to be settled and the opposing sides were very nearly equal, Mr. Taft's grandmother cast the deciding vote in favor of what was then considered the right side.

This was considered a valuable asset for Mr. Taft when aspiring to the Presidency of the United States. It illustrates the fact that women voted at the time of the formation of the Constitution of the United States and no discrimination was made against them.

The process of developing our states, gradually doing away with the qualifications, has been carried on slowly and because so few women in that early day were qualified to vote

it was assumed that they ought not to vote. And hence we
have the word "male" in our State Constitutions. But it is
contrary to the original design of the founders of this Republic. They were men inspired by a great idea, that of the
equality of the human race and the worth of the human being,
and they aimed to found a great Christian Republic in which
there should be "neither Jew nor Greek, nor bond nor free,
nor male nor female."

We have not yet realized their ideal but we are approaching it by slow degrees. Already six states have out-
grown all the forms of disfranchisement and given to women
equal rights with men, in making their wishes known in regard to public affairs.

The government by men alone has been far from successful. They themselves declare oft times that Democratic
institutions are a failure. That the Republic is going down.
One of our great statesmen was in the habit of saying that
"the Declaration of Independence and the Preamble to the
Constitution are glittering generalities." It is not uncommon
to hear men undervalue their right of suffrage and speak in
derogatory terms of our free institutions.

These are the confessions of the men themselves and
the misfortune of it is that what they say seems like truth,
but in fact we have not tried the Democratic institutions, nor
have we tested the value of a true Republic. Men and women
view subjects from different standpoints. Woman is interested first of all in the home and in the children and in the
social life around her. She, naturally, thinks first of the
philanthropies and all those instrumentalities which go to
make the home secure and which tend to a better development of child life.

Men, on the other hand, are interested in business.
The questions which appeal to them are financial questions.
They are questions of money. Our legislators give their attention very largely to purely money questions. Tariff and
taxes, banking and revenues, preservation of properties, ir-
rigation and sale of lands, or provisions for the care and
development of animals commend themselves to them because
to them all these things represent money and men view legislation from the money standpoint.

A few years ago our United States Government appropriated several million dollars to the investigation of the dis-

eases and conditions of hogs. It would be difficult to get
that amount of money appropriated for any commission having in view the consideration of the conditions which surround
our home life or the protection of child life. This is not because men value hogs so much but because the hog represents
money and the hogs of the country stand for a large amount
of money and men are interested in that side of the various
questions that concern the public weal.

Now when we have the business side represented and
the home and the philanthropies represented we may look for
a good government. But the effect of having only the money
side presented has been to place an undue value upon material things and has given rise to what we call the materialism
of our time.

We attach such great importance to the money power,
we bow down before the Golden Calf. We allow ourselves to
be governed by a dozen men who control the finances of the
whole country. A great many people today are complaining
of the supremacy of the wealthy classes and of their control
in our government and politics. And yet this is the direct
result of a masculine government in which the feminine influence has not been felt. The result is indeed disastrous.

As we feel ourselves today in the grip of a few men
holding hundreds of millions of property and controlling all
the business interest of our country we begin to realize the
necessity of an influence in the government which shall protect the home, which shall care for the children, which shall
look to the establishment of righteousness and truth and justice in our communities. This influence must come from the
women. It is only by their influence and their voices that
we can hope to secure a true Republic and save our nation
from premature destruction.

Already the people everywhere are rebelling against
the present condition of our political affairs. Already the
demagogue who boasts that he represents the progressive
element, that he stands for the people, is applauded and men
are ready to follow any kind of a leader that promises emancipation from the money power. But that emancipation can
only come by giving the ballot to all the people, by securing
the influence of women in favor of the great philanthropies,
in favor of those things that tend to building up purity and
truth in our communities. Woman Suffrage is the only possible salvation for this country.

Said Jack London, "Times change and men's minds change
with them. Down the past, civilizations have exposited themselves in terms of power, world power, other world power.
No civilization has yet exposited itself in terms of love for
man."

Our hope of permanent peace is based on the possibility of a civilization that will express itself in "terms of
love for man." The efforts that are now being made to secure peace by a League of Nations and otherwise all depend
upon force, all look to war to enforce peace. That is, they
will have peace if they have to fight for it. Such a peace
can only be temporary. No permanent peace is possible until men begin to think in terms of love for man, not until
they recognize the one God who hath made of "one blood all
nations of men for to dwell upon all the face of the earth."
Not, in short, until the people are educated in the doctrine
of the Fatherhood of God and the Brotherhood of man. The
acceptance of this doctrine can alone prepare people for such
a spirit of goodwill and friendliness as will make them desire peace instead of war.

President Wilson called upon our men to fight to make
the world safe for Democracy and it made every man of them
a hero. But Democracy is only one application to government
of the great principle of Brotherhood and Democracy can
never be "safe" until the doctrine of the worth of man is understood. Mr. Wilson has learned the value of Democracy;
he has yet to learn the foundation on which Democracy rests,
he has not yet learned the value of universal love. Only very
recently he has learned that women are a part of the human
race, he has yet to learn that all mankind of whatever name
or nation, race or condition are alike entitled to justice, opportunity, and liberty. He asks for "self-determination" for
small nations but not for "self-determination" for the individual. The right of every man and woman to life, liberty and
the pursuit of happiness he has not learned. The education

of experience will yet open to him the larger view of the
worth of man and when he recognizes the great principle we
may count upon his influence in freeing our political prisoners, in doing justice to the Indian and the Negro, in establishing equality for women; in fact, we may expect to attain
Democracy at home.

Had our government spent the one hundredth part of
the money in teaching the lesson of Brotherhood to the German people that it has spent in killing them, there would
have been no war. War is not possible where men recognize that all are alike God's Children, all the work of His
Hand and all precious in His Sight. Can we teach this great
lesson to the people of the warring world? True it will require time, it will be a matter of education to prepare the
way for such a civilization, but can we not begin today? We
have sacrificed fifty thousand men to make the world safe for
Democracy, can we not send one thousand consecrated preachers who shall teach the foundations of Democracy? Now is
the time to begin, when men are tired of war, when women
are heart-sick, when nations are impoverished and over bur-
dened, when all the people everywhere are wishing for something better. They will hear with satisfaction the new "Gospel of Peace on Earth, Good-will to men." Recently the
German government, in preparing a new system of education
for Prussia, instructed the school authorities that they should
promote the discussion of educational and "kultur" matters in
harmony with the new age. The new age! They are seeking
a new age, a new ideal, a new life, a new civilization, can
it not be a civilization of love instead of hate, a civilization
of brotherhood, a civilization of Peace? And the time of realization need not be so very long. Good is more contagious
than evil, truth is more acceptable than falsehood. If the
Peace Congress in preparing its constitution for a League of
Nations would insert a requirement that the Nations should be
instructed in the Christian doctrine of the Fatherhood of God
and the Brotherhood of man ten years hence would see a re-
formed world. The writer in a sermon recently preached at
the Universalist Church appealed to the denomination to make
itself a League for peace, by sending Missionaries to the old
world to "bind up the broken hearted" and to comfort those
who mourn." This doctrine of Brotherhood is their Creed.
They should go abroad to bind up the "broken hearted, to
proclaim liberty to the captives," to give unto them "beauty
for ashes, the oil of joy for mourning, the spirit of praise
for the garment of heaviness." What a glorious opportunity

for any denomination to be the exponent of a new civilization which should express itself in love for man! To make a new world in which men can dwell together in peace!

From <u>Suffragist</u>, pp. 213-214

We have achieved a great victory, the most important one
since the adoption of the Constitution of the United States,
the great instrument of which Gladstone said that it was the
greatest document ever composed by man. It was composed
by man and for man. It omitted woman altogether. Woman
was not born then. After a hundred and thirty-seven years
woman has been discovered. Slowly the work of emancipation has gone on. I recall the time, in 1861, when I circulated a petition throughout the city of Cleveland, Ohio. It
only asked for property rights and the guardianship of children, but it was bitterly opposed and men sneeringly said:
"You'll be wanting to vote next."

Six years after that came the great Kansas campaign!
For the first time in the history of the world the question of
woman's right to vote was submitted to a vote of the electors.
At that time I went to Kansas, and on the first day of July
1867, the first meeting of the campaign was held in Leaven-
worth. I traveled all over the state. I visited every city,
village and settlement. There were very few railroads, only
one or two stage routes, few livery stables, and almost no
roads of any kind. We made our way across the trackless
prairie. It was just after the Civil War, the people were
poor, and I came to them a missionary, empty-handed, dependent upon their good-nature for my conveyance from place
to place. It is to their credit that I spoke two or three times
every day in different places until the election in the autumn,
and I never missed an appointment.

Toward the last of September came Miss Anthony and
Mrs. Stanton, and later came George Francis Train, and altogether we did what could be done to win. But we met with
bitter opposition from the very men who had voted in the Legislature for the submission of the amendment. One month
before the election there was every indication that we should

win. The interest was great, women rode fifteen miles on horseback to attend the meetings, everything promised success. But just then the Republicans saw that we were in earnest and they began a violent opposition by lectures, circulars, ridicule and falsehood, and every influence which they could command. Consequently, when the election day came we had only one-third of all the votes cast. This was our first defeat.

After Two Defeats, Victory

Our second defeat came soon after. We had hoped that when the fourteenth amendment was drafted it would include women. But no, "the Negro's hour" was too precious to those politicians to be wasted upon women. They promised that when the Negro was enfranchised they would work for woman suffrage. However, it was quite generally supposed that voting was one of the "privileges and immunities" which the states were forbidden to "abridge." Many women beside Susan B. Anthony voted under the supposition that they were allowed to vote by the fourteenth amendment. But when the courts decided against us and Susan B. Anthony was fined, we knew that there was no hope in the amendments.

In 1869 a great victory startled the world and stirred the sleeping members of Congress, and they waked up and looked around. Wyoming with a constitution recognizing women asked for statehood! Heretofore the members of Congress had received our petitions, laughed at them, and put them away, but now they had the legislature of Wyoming to deal with and when they hesitated about receiving a state with a woman suffrage constitution word came to them from the Wyoming legislature: "We will stay out of the Union until the Day of Judgment, unless we come in with our women." It was our first great victory.

Convention in Washington

The same year, Susan B. Anthony began a series of conventions in Washington, which she kept up for twenty years, always appealing at every session to Congress, asking for an amendment to the constitution enfranchising women. They were great conventions, great in the earnestness they manifested, great in the enthusiasm they created, great in the numbers attending, when we consider the ignorance of the

people on the subject. Many came from curiosity, some
came to ridicule, and many "came to scoff but remained to
pray." But however they came, they heard the story of
equal rights for all, and the Woman Suffrage platform became the school of patriotism for the whole world. Mrs.
Stanton's wonderful eloquence, Miss Anthony's zeal, the wit
of Ernestine L. Rose, the historical arguments of Matilda
Joslyn Gage, and the legal lore of Belva Lockwood electri-
fied the nation, stirred the people everywhere, and gave them
a new idea of the meaning of liberty. These conventions laid
the foundation for the great movement in favor of woman's
emancipation.

In 1889 came the union of the National and American
societies. Mrs. Stanton was getting old and slow and Miss
Anthony was tired. The policy of the American association
was to work for suffrage in the states, and so the national
work for the amendment gave place, to a considerable extent,
to local state work. School suffrage, bond suffrage, presi-
dential suffrage, took the attention of the advocates of woman
suffrage, and some states gained suffrage by a referendum.
A few came in with suffrage in their constitutions.

Then ensued a period of indifference; people no longer
came to meetings from curiosity; ridicule had lost its force;
the stale old jokes no longer amused; no one came even to
scoff. And yet women kept on courageously working in all
possible ways, but apparently without success. Suffrage was
defeated unaccountably. No state had adopted woman suffrage
since 1894. Sometimes the legislatures refused to submit
the question, or it was defeated in the referendum. Politicians had passed the word along, "No more suffrage states."
The ten years preceding 1910 I have called the Great Desert
of woman suffrage. Of course women were working everywhere; the annual conventions of the National American Association were held, resolutions were passed, literature was
circulated and petitions were signed, but apparently without
result.

The Federal Suffrage Association kept up its hearings
before congressional committees. It presented bills and had
hearings in 1904, 1906 and some later, but nothing was done
and the outlook seemed dark. Susan B. Anthony had died in
1906 and no one had taken her place.

Suddenly and unexpectedly, help came out of the great
West. Washington voted for woman suffrage, carrying the

measure by a two-to-one vote! That marked a great epoch in
the history of woman suffrage. It was a light shining into the
darkness. There was great rejoicing. The states gained new
courage. State after state, stimulated by Washington's example, enfranchised its women.

Back Again in Congress

Then came Alice Paul and Lucy Burns, in 1913. I
remember the first letter they wrote me. They proposed to
establish headquarters in Washington and to push the amendment enfranchising women in Congress until victory was won.
I was delighted. It was the very thing I had proposed some
years previously in the executive board of the National-
American Woman Suffrage Association. My plan had been
sneered at and denounced as impossible and I had gone home,
crushed.

Miss Paul and Miss Burns worked faithfully and con-
tinuously and successfully. They organized the Woman's
Party. They did such thorough work as had never been done
before. They prepared a card index containing the names
of all the members of Congress and giving the political af-
filiation, religious views, and the social position of every
member. Having this, they had the members of the Federal
Association joined in appeals to Congress. Members of the
Woman's Party worked unceasingly. They picketed, they lectured, they went to jail, they suffered, they sacrificed, and,
all working together we conquered, and today we rejoice in
one of the greatest victories for humanity that has ever been
achieved.

Judge Walter Clark of the North Carolina Supreme
Court said in a letter to Miss Paul, dated March 5, 1920:
"The political history of the world shows no political capacity equal to that shown by the women in finally getting suffrage passed through Congress, by tenacity of purpose and
political skill in spite of bad faith of men who were pledged
to vote for you.... The feat of getting twenty-six special
sessions called up to date is one that no other power on the
planet could have accomplished. It will remain a marvel in
political history, that with the odds against you, you have
won or will soon have won, your enfranchisement. You certainly have earned it."

And Now?

And now, at the close of this long struggle, and when
the women of the whole United States are enfranchised, the
question arises, "What will the women do with their vote?"
The women of the nation, with ballots in their hands, must
do something effective for their country.   There still remain
many things to be done for women.   Justice in wages, in
law, and in public opinion has not been attained; and yet, ur-
gent as these subjects are, it seems to me that we should
first consider the great danger that threatens our country at
the present time.   The danger is militarism, the same which
we fought against Germany to destroy.   I could wish that the
whole womanhood of America would join and with one voice
denounce the whole military system, compulsory service,
military training, and the expenditure of millions of the people's money for munitions of war.   Surely the united voice
of all the women would be heard.   Militarism would be swept
away and our country consecrated to "peace on earth, good-
will to men."   Such an accomplishment would be worthy of
the great struggles and sacrifices that have been made to
give women the ballot.

A Sermon Preached in the Universalist Church,
Racine, Wis., by Rev. Olympia Brown

Text: "Life up your heads O ye gates and
be ye lifted up ye everlasting doors,"
--Psalm 24, Verse 7.

It is now nearly thirty years since I resigned my pastorate
in this church.   That is a long time and many things have
happened, but the grandest thing has been the lifting up of
the gates and the opening of the doors to the woman of America, giving liberty to twenty-seven million women, thus opening to them a new and larger life and a higher ideal.   The
future opens before them, fraught with great possibilities of
noble achievement.   It is worth a lifetime to behold the victory.   Then there have been other changes; Racine has grown
larger and richer and the population has changed; many have
come and some have gone.   The everlasting doors have opened
to some of our dearest and they have been permitted to behold the mysteries that lie beyond.   We see them no more.
We miss their ready cooperation and sympathy and love,
but we know that wherever they are, they are in God's universe and they are safe and all is well with them.   We have
had our struggles and our triumphs, our labors and our victories, our sorrows and our joys and some of us are growing old, but I would say in the words of Browning,

> Grow old along with me
> The best is yet to be,
> The last of life, for which the first was made;
> Our times are in His hand
> Who saith "A whole I planned,
> Youth shows but half; trust God, see all
> Nor be afraid.

Meantime, new proofs of the truths which we advocate
have been accumulating, sustaining the faith in which we have

lived, for which we have worked, and which has bound us together as a church.   New and wonderful evidences of the
truth of Universalism have come to us.   We formerly were
glad to be able to point to texts of Scripture as proof of our
doctrines, showing to the people the impossibility of an endless hell, telling them of the one God "who will have all men
to be saved and to come to the knowledge of the truth" and
assuring them that "As in Adam all die even so in Christ
shall all be made alive."

     We relied on the promises of revelation and we still
cherish these grand old texts.   They are dear to our hearts
and they will ever remain in our memories a precious possession.

     But now they are fortified and confirmed by the prom-
ises that come to us from nature "new every morning and
fresh every evening."   Today we are not dependent upon any
text or the letter of any book.   It is the spirit that giveth
life and the spirit speaks to our souls with every breath that
blows.   Science has been unravelling the mysteries of the
universe and has brought to light new examples of the Divine
power and purpose.   Burbank and Edison and Madame Curie
have lifted up the everlasting doors and revealed the Father's
countenance, all radiant with love.   Madame Curie, by working long in the laboratory has unlocked the rocks and released
radium, a substance fraught with incalculable benefit to humanity.   Creative chemistry has been at work and by its re-
actions and combinations has brought to light new powers in
the earth and in the air for the use of men.   We have not
half measured or understood the capabilities of this planet.
William Henry Perkins, a young boy of thirteen, became so
much interested in chemistry that he voluntarily gave up his
dinner and his noon hour to attend lectures on the subject.
He went on with his researches until he had discoveries in-
valuable to the manufacturer, among them that of aniline
dyes, and other things which have added wealth to the people.
Thus earth and air are filled with proofs of Divine love,
goodness and power.   The mountains and the hills have spoken
and the rocks and the soils have added their testimony.   "The
dynamic symmetries revealed in nature such as the form of
the fern leaf; the nautilus; and those vegetable products in
which the regular pentagon occurred or where we find a ge-
ometrical arrangement of leaves about a stalk" all show the
skillful handwork of the Divine, and all these wonderful scientific discoveries and revelations are proofs of God's unfailing love.   The Opening Doors lead to no dark dungeons, open

upon no burning lake, give no evidence of everlasting punishment. But all gladden us with assurances of Divine Goodness and indicate the final triumph of the good. "A charmed life old goodness, hath. The tares may perish, but the grain is not for death."

Not only by the researches of science are we shown the glories of creation, but the scenes of beauty which daily greet our eyes, the song of birds, fragrance of flowers, the moonlight shining on the waves all tell the same story of divine love. "The heavens declare the glory of God and the firmament showeth his handiwork." I have here a poem written by my mother in extreme old age in which the contemplation of the natural world seems to have lifted her above the weaknesses and pains of old age and enabled her to rise, in the entire confidence, into an atmosphere of Divine Love.

MORNING HYMN

From shades of night the morning woke;
Nature her hymn of praise began;
From all her keys the chorus broke,
Through all her chords the echoes ran.
  "Praise God" the roaring billow cried,
  The thunder's awful bass replied.
In dulcet tones of music sweet
Each lowly flower its fragrance lent;
Birds sang, the morning light to greet,
And every bough in homage bent.
  The sun arose in majesty;
  Nature in worship bent the knee.
Roll on, sweet harmonies of love.
Through all earth's blooming valleys, roll;
Above the world, the stars above,
Soars upward my enraptured soul.
  Borne on devotion's wing of fire,
  To Nature's God my thoughts aspire.

But more significant than even the voices of the natural world is the evidence of Divine life which we see in man himself. When a great heroic deed is done humanity is lifted up and ennobled and we have the assurance that there is a spirit in man and the Lord God giveth him understanding. Oh, what grand acts of self-sacrifice and high courage, what heroism, have we seen in innumerable instances during the last few sorrowful years, all showing that there is a soul in

man partaking of the Divine life. A thousand instances of
depravity are forgotten in our admiration of one great heroic
action by which human nature is lifted to a higher level, by
which we know that man has a soul which is immortal and
which enables him to utilize and make his own the wonderful
resources with which the earth with all its glories is fitted
up for his uses.

When the other day I saw crowds of women of all conditions coming into the polling booth all filled with great enthusiasm, forgetting old prejudices, old associations and
former interest, only seeking to know how to serve the state,
ready to leave their usual amusements and associations and
give themselves to new subjects of study, not to serve any
particular party, but only to learn how to help the world I
said, they are grander than I thought. They have "meat to
eat that the world knows not of," there is a Divine Life in
them which this new experience is revealing.

The greatness of men, the grand capabilities of women
attest the worth of the human being fashioned in the image of
God.

It is true that the ignorance of men and the awful mistakes they make, the wrongs they do and the sins they commit, bringing with them, even here, terrible punishment and
embittering life, might cause us to doubt were it not that we
see that there is a pardoning power in the spiritual world as
there is healing in nature.

The riven rock soon covers itself with moss and becomes a thing of beauty. The tree deformed and disfigured
puts out new twigs and branches and covers itself with ver-
dure and so the warped and travel-stained, sorrow-stricken
souls of men shall at last put on the garments of Holiness.
Men shall find remedies for their weakness, enlightenment
for their ignorance and so rise out of their degradation and
their sin.

One of our noted political prisoners said the other
day in an interview, "I have never been more hopeful and
more confident of the future than I am today. Nor have I
ever had so great faith in the moral order of the universe
as I have today."

"There is a kinship of misery that generates the true
sweetness of human nature, the very milk of human kind-

ness." Thus the sins of men and their sorrows come at last
to confirm the great truths revealed in the natural world.

And so Science: the beauties of nature and the grand
possibilities of humanity furnish overwhelming proofs of the
final victory of the good and the ultimate purification of every
human soul.

And this is Universalism: the grandest system of religious truth that has ever been revealed to man. The doctrine for which the world waits.

A short time ago a correspondent of the Nation wrote
to the editor begging him to publish something hopeful. He
said he was so tired of being discouraged; he longed for something hopeful. And he spoke for thousands who in this time
of uncertainty and chaos and confusion are longing for a ray
of light, something to relieve the discouragements of the hour.

Mothers all over this land who have heard the solemn
tidings that their sons have been slaughtered on the battlefield; wives who have been robbed of everything--companion-
ship, support, all the joys of life; multitudes whom the terrible pictures of suffering and torture have filled with horror,
he spoke for all of these.

ALL NEED MORE HOPE, ETERNAL HOPE.

Hope! When I mourn, with sympathizing mind,
The wrongs of fate, the woes of human kind,
Thy blissful omens bid my spirit see
The boundless fields of rapture yet to be;
I watch the wheels of Nature's mazy plan,
And learn the future by the past of man.

He spoke for the whole world that is longing for hope,
and Universalism is the answer to that cry, for this the world
waits.

Oh Lift up your heads, O ye gates, even lift them up
ye everlasting doors, that the King of Glory may come in.
The Lord mighty in love, rich in tender mercies, abundant
in pardoning power. He comes to bring consolation to the
sorrowful, inspiration to the toiler, hope for the sinner. He
comes to bless the world and to help humanity to rise out of
its selfishness and ignorance.

We talk of reforms. We have hoped to make the world

safe for democracy; to establish a league of peace; but the
very first necessity in reform work is the recognition of Divine capabilities in man.   The foundation of democracy is the
realization that every human being is a child of God, entitled
to the opportunities of life, worthy of respect, and requiring
an atmosphere of justice and liberty for his development.

We can never make the world safe for democracy by
fighting.   Rather by showing the power of Justice done to
each humble individual shall we be able to create a firm basis for the state.   We can establish a league of peace only
by teaching the nations the great lesson of the Fatherhood of
God and the Brotherhood of Man.

Every nation must learn that the people of all the nations are children of God and must all share the wealth of
the world.   You may say that this is impracticable, far away,
and can never be accomplished.   But this is the work which
Universalists are appointed to do.   Universalists sometimes,
somehow, somewhere, must ever teach this great lesson.

We are not alone.   There is always an unseen power
working for righteousness.   The Infinite is behind us.   The
eternal years of God are ours.

And that is the message which I bring to you today.
Stand by this great faith which the world needs and which you
are called to proclaim.

It is not necessary to go far away to tell the story of
God's love or even to win the nations.   God has given us the
heathen for an inheritance.   Here they come to our own city
from far away countries and from the islands of the ocean.
And here in Racine we may illustrate the great principles of
our faith by our charity, by our kindliness and consideration
for all.   We shall speak the language of Universal love and
it will be heard and the message will be carried far and wide.

What signifies that your numbers are few today when
you are inspired by truths that are everlasting and have before you ever the vision of final victory, the assurance of the
salvation of all souls?

Universalism shall at last win the world.

Dear Friends, stand by this faith.   Work for it and
sacrifice for it.   There is nothing in all the world so impor-

tant to you as to be loyal to this faith which has placed before you the loftiest ideals, which has comforted you in sorrow, strengthened you for noble duty and made the world beautiful for you. Do not demand immediate results but rejoice that you are worthy to be entrusted with this great message and that you are strong enough to work for a great true principle without counting the cost. Go on finding ever new applications of these truths and new enjoyments in their contemplation, always trusting in the one God which ever lives and loves. "One God, one law, one element, and one far-off divine event to which the whole creation moves."

A. SELECTED PRINTED WORKS BY BROWN

> The richest source for the study of Olympia
> Brown is the Olympia Brown Papers in the
> Schlesinger Library on the History of Women,
> Radcliffe College. This voluminous collection
> contains hundreds of entries most of which are
> in manuscript or typescript form.

"Accepting the Test," Woman's Journal (Boston), May 26, 1877.

Acquaintances, Old and New, Among Reformers. Milwaukee: S. E. Tate Printing Co., 1911.

Autobiography. Boston: Universalist Historical Society, 1963.

"Christian Charity: A Doctrinal Sermon for Universalists," Gospel Banner (Augusta, Me.), March 30, 1872.

"Crime and the Remedy," An address delivered before the Parliament of Religions at the Hall of Columbus, Art Institute, Chicago, Sept. 22, 1893. Olympia Brown Papers (OBP), II, 29.

Democratic Ideals: A Memorial Sketch of Clara B. Colby. Federal Suffrage Association, 1917.

"Do We Need More Parishes?" Star in the West (Cincinnati, Ohio), Oct. 11, 1877.

"Do We Need More Parishes?" (2) Star in the West (Cincinnati, Ohio), Oct. 18, 1877.

"The Dozing Captains," Star in the West (Cincinnati, Ohio), Sept. 13, 1877.

"Ecclesiastical Trials," Star in the West (Cincinnati, Ohio), Jan. 24, 1878.

"Ecclesiastical Trials," (2) Star in the West (Cincinnati, Ohio), March 14, 1878.

"Equality of Rights Is All the Negro Asks," The Public (April 9, 1904), pp. 13-14.

"Ex-Pastors," Star in the West (Cincinnati, Ohio), March 27, 1878.

"The Forty Ministers," Star in the West (Cincinnati, Ohio), Sept. 20, 1877.

"Hand of Fellowship," in Services at the Ordination and Installation of Rev. Phebe A. Hanaford. Boston: C. C. Roberts, 1870, pp. 29-31.

"Have We a Right to Die?" Star in the West (Cincinnati, Ohio), August 30, 1877.

"Have We a Right to Live?" Star in the West (Cincinnati, Ohio), August 23, 1877.

"The Higher Education of Women," Repository, vol. 51 (Feb. 1874), pp. 81-86.

"The Men of Seventy-Six," Manford's New Monthly Magazine, vol. 20, no. 5 (May 1876), pp. 197-201.

"Occasional Sermon," Gospel Banner (Augusta, Me.), Sept. 28, 1872.

"The Opening Doors," Sermon preached in the Universalist Church, Racine, Wisconsin, Sept. 12, 1920. OBP, II, 36.

"The Pastoral Relation," Star in the West (Cincinnati, Ohio), July 5, 1877.

"Reminiscences of a Pioneer," The Suffragist (Sept. 1920), pp. 213-214.

"Speech," in Report of the Convention for Organization: Woman's National Liberal Union, ed. by Matilda Gage. Syracuse, N.Y.: Masters and Stone, 1890, pp. 53-56.

"Two or Three Planks," Wisconsin Citizen (March 1889).

"United States Citizenship," Address delivered before the government Congress of the World's Exposition, Chicago, Aug. 9, 1893. OBP, II, 29.

"We Have a Right to Die, " Star in the West (Cincinnati, Ohio), Sept. 6, 1877.

"We Should All Pull Together, " Wisconsin Citizen (Feb. 1890).

"Where Is the Mistake?" The Woman's Tribune (March 8, 1890).

"Why the Church Should Demand the Ballot for Women, " n.d. printed. OBP, II, 49.

"Wisconsin, " in History of Woman Suffrage, ed. by S. B. Anthony and Ida Husted Harper. Rochester, N.Y.: S. B. Anthony, 1902, vol. 4, pp. 988-993.

"Woman and Skepticism, " The Alpha, vol. 10, no. 7 (March 1, 1885), pp. 1-5.

"Woman's Place in the Church, " The Monthly Religious Magazine (July 1869), pp. 26-35.

"Woman's Suffrage," Address delivered at the Rockford Fair, Aug. 29, 1888. Reported in the Rockford (Ill.) Star. OBP, II, 29. Papers, II, 29.

B. WORKS ABOUT BROWN

Graves, Lawrence. "Olympia Brown, " Notable American Women. Cambridge, Mass.: Harvard Univ. Press, 1971, pp. 256-58.

Hanaford, Phebe. Daughters of America. Boston: B. B. Russell, 1883, pp. 425-26.

Hanson, E. R. "Olympia Brown," in Our Woman Workers: Biographical Sketches of Women Eminent in the Universalist Church for Literary, Philanthropic and Christian Work. Chicago: The Star and Covenant Office, 1882, pp. 427-32.

Hitchings, Catherine F. "Olympia Brown, " in Universalist and Unitarian Women Ministers. Boston: The Universalist Historical Society, 1975, pp. 30-31.

Miller, Russell E. "God Bless and Make Us Grateful for Our Women," in The Larger Hope: The First Century of the Universalist Church in America, 1770-1870. Boston: Unitarian-Universalist Assc., 1979, pp. 534-73.

Neu, Charles E. "Olympia Brown and the Woman's Suffrage Movement," Wisconsin Magazine of History, vol. 43, no. 4 (Summer 1960), pp. 277-87.

Schmidt, Ralph. "The Message of Olympia Brown, Preacher," Today's Speech, vol. 12, no. 2 (April 1964).

_____. "Olympia Brown," The Christian Universalist, vol. II, no. 3 (Fall 1963), pp. 3-4.

_____. "Olympia Brown's Unitarian Christian Belief," Unitarian Christian, vol. 19, no. 2 (1964), pp. 19-25.

_____. "Olympia Brown: Two Sermons--Introduction," Annual Journal of the Universalist Historical Society, vol. 4 (1963), pp. 93-110.

_____. "Sermon by Olympia Brown," Christian Universalist, vol. 2, no. 4 (Winter 1963), pp. 2-4.